THE CIA INSIDER'S GUIDE TO THE
IRAN CRISIS

From CIA Coup to the Brink of War

T0064841

Gareth Porter and John Kiriakou

Skyhorse Publishing

Skyhorse Publishing books may be purchased in bulk at special discounts for sales promotion, corporate gifts, fund-raising, or educational purposes. Special editions can also be created to specifications. For details, contact the Special Sales Department, Skyhorse Publishing, 307 West 36th Street, 11th Floor, New York, NY 10018 or info@skyhorsepublishing.com.

Skyhorse® and Skyhorse Publishing® are registered trademarks of Skyhorse Publishing, Inc.®, a Delaware corporation.

Visit our website at www.skyhorsepublishing.com.

10 9 8 7 6 5 4 3 2 1

Library of Congress Cataloging-in-Publication Data is available on file.

ISBN: 978-1-5107-5609-0
eBook: 978-1-5107-5616-8

Cover design by Kai Texel

Printed in the United States of America

Table of Contents

Authors' Note

Preface

AFTER FORTY YEARS OF UNREMITTINGLY OFFICIAL U.S. hostility toward the Islamic Republic of Iran through seven different administrations, the United States is closer than ever before to war with Iran. After a nuclear agreement with Iran that appeared to offer a chance for a softening of U.S.-Iran conflict in 2015, the Trump administration has turned the clock back to the days of the George W. Bush administration, when Vice-President Dick Cheney and his neoconservative staff were dead set on attacking the Islamic Republic.

In fact, the risk of war with Iran is now far more serious than it was during those dangerous days of Bush-Cheney policy toward Iran. Like Bush, Trump himself doesn't want to go to war, but he has allowed to a team of extreme right-wingers with ties to Israel's Likud Party and the Christian Zionists to take over the formulation of U.S. Iran policy. Their strategy was aimed at entangling Trump in a war with Iran, and they came very close to succeeding in 2019.

Trump managed to dodge that threat, but to step back from the brink of war, he must go further to address the real ticking time bomb of his adminis- tration—the attack on Iran's right to export its oil to its long-time customers across Europe and Asia. Iran cannot and will not accept that U.S. aggression, and eventually it will take action that would likely trigger an escalation that quickly turn into U.S.-Iran War. That war could spread across the entire Middle East and bring chaos in its wake.

This book explains clearly and in detail for the first time why the pres- ent U.S. Iran policy represents a very serious threat to Americans and how and how the United States got itself into such a situation. It shows how the U.S. policy toward Iran going all the way back to the CIA's overthrow of Iranian Prime Minister Mohamed Mossadegh in 1953 has remained mired in a stubborn insistence on denying Iran's most basic rights as an indepen- dent nation-state. And it explains how U.S. policy has fallen prey to false narratives about both the nuclear issue and Iran's support for "terrorism" and "destabilization" of the Middle East that must be corrected in order to find a path out of the present morass of U.S. Iran policy.

We have come to this task from different paths—John from being a covert CIA operations veteran who resisted pressure to go along with the Agency's post-9/11 torture program, Gareth from long years as an independent journalist investigating false narratives surrounding U.S. Iran policy as well as America's wars. We are united in hoping that this book will contribute to greater public understanding of the need for fundamental change in the present policy and for making peace with Iran.

1. From CIA Coup to Islamic Republic

Before the Americans:
Iran's Encounter with Imperialism

ONE OF THE REASONS THE UNITED States has stumbled into disastrous wars over the past half century is the ignorance of successive generations of policymakers about the nations they have sought to subdue. U.S. officials have systematically failed to understand the force of their adversaries' nationalism and the importance of their historical memories of resistance to imperialism.

The importance of that factor could hardly be clearer in the case of Iran, which is one of the oldest nations on earth with the strongest feelings of nationalism and resentment of foreign domination. Archeological finds from northern Iran date from the fifth millennium BC, and through the Median, Archaemenid, Seleucid, Parthian, and Sasanian empires document the cultural sophistication and proud history of the Persian people. The Iranian national identity was so well-established by the time of the poet Ferdowsi's tenth century epic Shahnameh that it referred explicitly to Iran more than a thousand times.[1]

Iran has a very long history of being victimized by aggressive imperialism on the part of both Russia and Britain. Between 1804 and 1813, and again from 1826 to 1828, Czarist Russia invaded Iran and seized what became the present-day Russian republic of Dagestan, as well as what have become the

---

1. Ervand Abrahamian, *A History of Modern Iran* (Cambridge: Cambridge University Press, 2008), 2.

independent nations of Georgia, Armenia, and Azerbaijan.[2] Russia imposed economic domination on Iran through the Treaty of Turkomanchai in 1828, which took way Iran's power to set tariffs and allowed Russia to obtain a wide range of economic concessions and colonial privileges from the corrupt Qajar dynasty.

The British and other European powers later demanded the same rights. Import duties on consumer goods were set so low as to allow foreign goods to flood the Iranian market. The Iranian consumer goods industry collapsed, and Iran's trade balance was in crisis. In response the Iranian court and its landowning allies rapidly converted land previously devoted to subsistence food crops to cash crops for export. The primary such new cash crop was opium, which had become the leading Iranian cash crop by the 1870s. It was after that shift from subsistence to cash crops that the Great Famine of 1870-72 occurred, causing as many 1.5 million Iranians deaths—15 to 25 percent of the population. Historians have debated the relative importance of different causes of that death toll, in part because landowners, merchants and bureaucrats hoarded grain supplies to amass fortunes. Nevertheless, it is widely believed by Iranians that the loss of control over the Iranian economy to imperialist powers, through their hold on a weakened Qajar royal court, was a major factor in the ferocity of the famine.[3]

The British took advantage of the feeble Qajar dynasty to turn most of Iran into what the British considered a "semi-colony"—a colony in all but name. In 1972, the Qajar ruler, Nasir al-Din Shah, gave Baron Julius de Reuter (the founder of Reuters News Agency) control over most of Iran's mines, all of its railway construction, its irrigation networks and other agricultural and industrial projects in Iran. And in 1890, a British military officer obtained monopoly control over all production, sale and export of Iran's tobacco crop, impoverishing Iranian producers. The tobacco monopoly provoked a remarkable demonstration of political resistance in 1891, when

---

2. William Bayne Fisher; P. Avery, P.;, G.R.G. Hambly; C. Melville. *The Cambridge History of Iran.* Cambridge: Cambridge University Press, 1991), 7.
3. Charles Melville, "Persian Famine of 1870–1872: Prices and Politics", Disasters, Overseas Development Institute, Vol. 12, no. 4, (December 1988), 309–325; Nikki R. Keddie, "Iranian Revolutions in Comparative Perspective," *American Historical Review*, 88 (1983): 379–98; Ram Baruch Regavim, "The Most Sovereign of Masters: The History of Opium in Modern Iran", PhD Diss., University of Pennsylvania, 2012, 31-32, 62-64.

Iranians stopped using tobacco almost completely in response to a religious edict, forcing the Shah to rescind the concession.[4]

British foreign minister Lord Curzon later referred to "the most complete and extraordinary surrender of the entire industrial resources of a kingdom into foreign hands that had probably ever been dreamt of."[5] That sweeping description was clearly meant to include the concession that would come to define Iranian anti-imperialism in the twentieth century: the 60-year oil concession granted to a British citizen in 1901 covering the entire country except for the five northern-most provinces.

It was not merely the appropriation of Iran's oil resources by a British entrepreneur that shaped the ultimate Iranian political response but the company's blatant cheating of Iran out of the share of the profits due it under the agreement once oil was discovered in 1908. The owner set up an entirely new company and sold all its production, refining and marketing rights to it, so the Iranian state could not get even the paltry 10 percent share of profits the agreement had called for.[6]

A new educated middle class that had absorbed liberal Western political ideas carried out a "Constitutional Revolution" in 1905, the centerpiece of which was the end of the absolutism of the Qajar monarchy and the establishment of an Iranian legislature or Majles. One of the first decisions by the new Majles was to appoint American lawyer and financial adviser William Morgan Shuster as "Treasurer-General" to help Iran establish a modern financial system as a tool to begin to break down the British and Russian grip on the country's economy.

Shuster had an ambitious plan to create a "gendarmerie" of tax collectors in order to give the Iranian constitutional monarchy a financial basis for such independence. But the Russians had no intention of allowing such a subversion of its extraordinary control over the court. In a blatant move to deepen their semi-colonial control of Iran, Russia and Britain signed the

4. Nikki R. Keddie. *Religion and Rebellion in Iran: The Tobacco Protest of 1891-92* (London: Frank Cass, 1966), 1-6; Roy Muttahedeh, *The Mantle of the Prophet: Religion and Politics in Iran* (Oxford: Oneworld, 2000), 215.
5. Nader Hashemi, "Donald Trump and the Strangling of Persia," Al Jazeera, July 11, 2019. https://www.aljazeera.com/indepth/opinion/donald-trump-strangling-persia-190710142907968.html.
6. "Nationalization of the Iranian Oil Industry—An Outline of Its Origins and Issues," Confidential report, World Bank, February 19, 1952, declassified from World Bank archives January 11, 2012. http://pubdocs.worldbank.org/en/608151403270477052/wbg-archives-1806440.pdf. This report is the most comprehensive, detailed and penetrating account of the history that led to the nationalization of the British oil company available to the public.

Anglo-Russian Convention of 1907, which delineated exclusive zones of economic exploitation for the Russians in the north (including Tehran), and the British in the south. It also created a buffer zone in the rest of the country in which both powers could carry out economic activities freely. When the Russians got wind of Shuster's plan they issued an ultimatum to the Majles demanding his firing, and then in 1911 sent troops to occupy their zone.[7] Upon his return to the United States, Shuster wrote a book on his experiences with the title *The Strangling of Persia*, describing how the Russian and British control had systematically prevented Iran's economic and political development.[8]

During World War I, the Ottomans attacked and occupied Iran, because Iran was allied with the west, while the Ottoman Turks had thrown their lot in with the Germans. The British drove the Ottomans out in 1916, but from 1917 to 1919, another terrible famine combined with disease epidemics caused a death toll estimated at from 2 million to as many as 8 million—from 10 to 40 percent of the population. The famine had multiple causes, but the number of deaths from starvation was magnified by British policies of purchasing grain in the area where it was already scarce to support British troops in Iran and Mesopotamia, and by failing to bring in more foodstuffs from India or Mesopotamia in order to save shipping space for war materiel.[9]

With the defeat of Germany and the Bolshevik revolution in Russia, the British were in a position to press for the full integration of Iran into the empire. A proposed Anglo-Persian Agreement of 1919 gave Britain the sole right to provide Iran with loans, arms, military instructors, and customs administrators, along with monopoly over railway construction. But the

---

7. Abrahamian, *A History of Modern Iran*, 55, 58.
8. W. Morgan Shuster, *The Strangling of Persia* (New York: The Century Co., 2012). For a PDF of the complete original book, see http://www.culturaldiplomacy.org/academy/pdf/research/books/public_diplomacy/The_Strangling_Of_Persia_-_W._Morgan_Shuster.pdf.
9. Muhammad Gholi Majd, *The Great Famine and Genocide in Persia* (Lanham, Md.: University Press of America, 2014), 1-3. Majd's estimate of death of 8-10 million from starvation has been sharply criticized by some scholars, who believed it was vastly exaggerated and that epidemics account for most of the two million deaths that they estimate for the period. See Mahmood Messkoub, "Social Policy in Iran in the Twentieth Century". Iranian Studies. 2006, 39 (2): 227–252; Ervand Abrahamian, The Coup: 1953, The CIA and the Roots of Modern U.S.-Iran Relations (New York and London: The New Press, 2013), 27.

Iranian political atmosphere was so strongly hostile to the British presence that no Iranian figure could be found who would approve the agreement.[10]

Finally, in February 1921, Reza Khan, the commander of a nearby Iranian Cossack garrison, seized control of Tehran in a British-supported military coup and created a military dictatorship. In 1925 Reza Khan declared himself Shah, or monarch, beginning the Pahlavi Dynasty as Reza Shah. For the next fifteen years, Reza Shah carried out a genuine process of state-building, creating a government that reasserted governmental authority over the country's tribes and provinces. One of his first moves was to bring in another American, Arthur Millspaugh, to create an effective tax system. This time, with the full support of the new Persian strongman, the American soon built a modern tax and fiscal system, enabling the emerging state to present its first annual comprehensive budget. By 1941, the state's revenues had increased by 15 times compared to their 1925 level.[11]

But in 1933 Reza Shah could not resist the power of the British-owned oil company when it demanded a major revision of the original 1901 concession, which it had systematically violated by failing to pay any royalties whatsoever for years on one pretext or another. The Iranian government was forced to sign a new agreement with the Anglo-Persian Oil Company, despite having identified 13 distinct ways that it was much less favorable than the original concession. The British mobilized their forces, threatening to occupy southern Iran and to create puppet sheikdoms throughout the concession. The result was that the British obtained an extension of the concession for 32 more years until 1993, with a paltry annual royalty payment to the government that did not reflect the certainty of a future rise in the value of the oil.[12] That agreement became a symbol of British imperialism in Iran that increasingly stirred popular anti-British nationalism over the next two decades.

During World War II, both the Soviet Union and Britain occupied zones in the north and south of Iran, respectively, that were similar to their zones of control during the period of their joint imperialist domination over Iran in the 19th and early 20th centuries. The allies feared that Reza Shah would be favorable to Germany and forced him into exile, whereupon his eldest son, Mohamaed Reza Pahlavi, became the Shah of Iran at 21 years of age.

---

10. A. R. Begli Beigie, "Repeating mistakes: Britain, Iran & the 1919 Treaty," *The Iranian*, March 27, 2001. http://www.iranian.com/History/2001/March/Britain/index.html.

11. Abrahamian, *A History of Modern Iran*, 63-69.

12. "Anglo-Persian Oil Company," *Encyclopaedia Iranica.* http://www.iranicaonline.org/articles/anglo-persian-oil-company.

After the war, the Soviet Union tried to exploit its military presence as bargaining leverage to negotiate its own oil concession with the Iranian government. The Soviets promised not to use such a concession as an excuse to maintain forces in Iran, and Iran agreed to a bi-national company for developing oil in the northern region, but made it conditional on approval by the Majles. But after Moscow did withdraw all its troops from Iranian territory by May 1946, the Majles, no longer willing to give up control of over its oil resources to any foreign power, refused to approve it.[13]

The CIA Defeats Iranian Nationalism

BY THE EARLY POST-WAR YEARS, THE demand for nationalization of the Anglo-Iranian Oil Company (AOIC) had become the central issue in Iranian politics. The Iranian public was well aware that the 1933 agreement was blatantly unfair, depriving Iran of a fair share of the income from the company's sales. And Iranians were no longer willing to tolerate the company's unwillingness to share its extremely large profits equitably, its mistreatment of its Iranian workers and insistence that only British could fill skilled jobs.[14]

In fact, the working conditions for the company's unskilled workers were scandalous. The British labor attaché admitted that most of those workers lived in tents that had no proper wooden floors. When the company announced cuts in rental allowances for oil workers in March 1951 it sparked protests and a general strike that continued for weeks and involved more than 50,000 oil workers. Their calls for nationalization raised the popular political demand to a new level.[15]

Muhammad Mossadegh was the pivotal political figure in Iran's struggle for control over its own resources—and the most tragic figure in modern Iranian political history. His father had been Finance Minister during the Qajar Dynasty, and his mother was a princess. He studied political science in

13. Despatch From the Embassy in Iran to the Department of State, February 23, 1951, Foreign Relations of the United States, 1952-1954, Iran, 1951-1954. https://history.state.gov/historicaldocuments/frus1951-54Iran/d1.
14. Mostafa Elm, *Oil, Power and Principle: Iran's Oil Nationalization and its Aftermath* (Syracuse: Syracuse University Press, 1992, 49.
15. Ervand Abhramian, *The Coup: 1953, the CIA, and the Roots of Modern U.S.-Iranian Relations* (New York: The New Press, 2013), 62-72.

Paris and, in 1913, he became the first Iranian to earn a PhD from a European university. He was elected to parliament, but went into self-imposed exile in Switzerland to protest the Anglo-Persian Treaty of 1919. In 1920, however, he returned to Iran to become Minister of Justice and Governor of Fars Province. A year later he became Finance Minister, and then in 1923, Minister of Foreign Affairs and Governor of Azerbaijan. He was reelected to parliament that same year.[16]

Mossadegh was Iran's "Mr. Clean," with a record opposing corruption and nepotism and fighting against British domination. In 1949, he co-founded the National Front of Iran, a political party dedicated to establishing democracy and ending foreign interference in Iranian politics, with nationalization of the British oil monopoly as the new party's explicit goal. He was immensely popular in the parliament, and on April 28, 1951 he was nominated as Prime Minister by a vote of 79-12. His nomination was immediately celebrated with demonstrations in cities around the country.

The first order of business for Mossadegh's new government was to nationalize the Anglo-Iranian Oil Company (AOIC). The month before his election the Majles had voted unanimously to demand government action on a Commission's recommendation for nationalization. Mossadegh immediately set in motion the process of nationalizing the AOIC and creating Iran's own national oil company.

Publicly the AOIC claimed that the nationalization was illegal, because it violated the 1933 agreement, and that it had made serious proposals to increase the share of profits going to Iran and even offered a 50/50 sharing of profits. The British government openly intervened in the dispute, arguing that the Iranians were incapable of managing the oil industry and could not be relied on to maintain production, and warning that oil might not be available to the rest of the world. The British and Anglo-American media gave the public a cartoon portraying Mossadegh himself as childish, unstable, extremist and psychologically incapable of compromise.

But it was all a calculated propaganda ploy to obscure the British determination to maintain their control over Iranian resources as a prop for Britain's waning global power and to continue the enormous profits the concession was generating by cheating Iran out of hundreds of billions of dollars. Privately the British cited the danger that ceding control to the Iranians would threaten nationalizations of a long list of highly valued commodities

---

16. Gholam Reza Afkhami, *The Life and Times of the Shah* (Berkeley: University of California Press, 2009), 110.

then under British control in South and Southeast Asia, Latin America and even Greece.[17]

A confidential 1952 World Bank study on the nationalization issue acknowledged that the Mossadegh government had a compelling case for nationalization, starting with the fact that the 1933 agreement, which was far more unfavorable to the government's interests than the original concession, was signed "under duress". It pointed out that, when the Iranians had refused to accept the unjust demands by the company, the British Navy in the Persian Gulf had made preparations for a possible occupation of southern Iran, and the British had threatened to set up a puppet sheikhdom in the area where oilfields were located.[18]

The confidential World Bank report observed that the Iranian government had learned from decades of experience with the company that it would never honestly carry out any agreement but would always find multiple ways to cheat Iran out of to its share of the profits. The report endorsed the Mossadegh government's argument that nationalization was necessary for Iran's economic development. The British Company had exploited is "political and economic control" over oil operations, and had used its influence to retard Iran's economic development by discouraging the development of other Iranian industries, which kept Iranian labor dependent on the Company, thus reducing its costs.[19]

The British couldn't legally challenge the right of Iran to nationalize its oil; instead they insisted that fair compensation had to be based on the value of the oil far into the future. The Mossadegh government rejected that principle, which would have kept Iran in debt indefinitely. The AOIC, with British government support, exploited every form of power it had to force the hand of the Mossadegh government. The AIOC ordered the entire expatriate staff to resign, and London pressured other European governments to make it virtually impossible for any other expatriates to work for the nationalized company. Finally, it imposed a blockade on all Iranian oil export and in June 1952 impounded a tanker that dared to leave Iran with what the British called "stolen" oil. Finally, the British military devised a new plan

---

17. Abrahamian, *The Coup*, 88.
18. "Nationalization of the Iran Oil Industry—An Outline of Its Origin and Issues", confidential World Bank study, no author shown, February 19, 1952, Declassified from World Bank Archives January 11, 2012, 12-13. http://pubdocs.worldbank.org/en/608151403270477052/wbg-archives-1806440.pdf.
19. "Nationalization of the Iranian Oil Industry," 33

for the occupation of the oil industry center in Abadan aptly code-named "Buccaneer".[20]

The Truman administration could not deny the immense popularity of Mossadegh's anti-colonial nationalist message within Iran. During his visit to Iran in 1952 Averell Harriman, Special Assistant to President Harry Truman, observed in a message to Washington, "[T]here is complete unanimity among qualified American officials that Mossadegh is strongly supported by a very large majority of Iranian people, and no Iranian program has ever been backed to the extent of his program to eliminate British influence in Iran and nationalize the oil industry."[21]

But the United States was unwilling to abandon its alliance with the British whose continued colonial and semi-colonial power was seen as a necessary to the U.S. global power position in the Cold War with the Soviet Union. That meant that the United States had to support continued British control over Iran's oil resources. In an April 1951 meeting of senior U.S. and British officials in Washington, both sides had been in full agreement that "effective power should be kept over this valuable asset."[22]

After the British Embassy left Iran in November 1952 the British Ambassador in Washington sought State Department support for the idea of a coup against Mossadegh. He thought the best tactic in selling Washington on the plan was to play on the presumed U.S. fear of a Communist takeover. The Ambassador argued that Mossadegh was "very unlikely to do anything effective against the communists"—referring to the pro-Soviet Tudeh Party—because Mossadegh was "too vacillating to take a strong stand."[23]

In his first two months in office, however, President Dwight D. Eisenhower contemplated—for the first time in U.S. policy toward the nationalization issue—actually breaking with the British hard line toward Mossadegh. His thinking was certainly influenced by a new CIA national intelligence estimate concluding that the Mossadegh government "has the capability to take effective repressive action to check mob violence and Tudeh agitation and will probably continue to act against specific challenges of this sort as they arise." It

---

20. Abrahamian, *The Coup*, 111-112.
21. The Special Assistant to the President (Harriman) to the Department of State, July 19, 1951, Foreign Relations of the United States, Middle East 1952-1954, Iran 1951-1954. https://history.state.gov/historicaldocuments/frus1952-54v10/d44.
22. Abrahamian, *The Coup*, 83.
23. State Department Memorandum of Conversation, "British Proposal to Organize a Coup d'Etat in Iran," Top Secret, December 3, 1952, National Security Archive, George Washington University. https://nsarchive2.gwu.edu//dc.html?doc=3914380-02-State-Department-Memorandum-of-Conversation.

further predicted that the Mossadegh government "almost certainly desires to keep US support as a counterweight to the USSR and appears to want US economic and military assistance" and would likely blame the United States for the deterioration of the economy because of British intransigence.[24]

Eisenhower presided over a National Security Council meeting on March 4, 1953 that discussed two policy options based on those premises. One option was to disassociate the United States from the unpopular British oil policy to encourage the British to settle; the other was to purchase oil from Mossadegh's nationalized National Iranian Oil Company, supply the company with technicians to replace some of the foreigners who had quit, and provide economic aid to the Mossadegh regime.

Secretary of State John Foster Dulles expressed doubt about the two options because of his concern about not alienating the British, with whom the United States was still closely allied elsewhere in issues related to anti-Western nationalism. But Eisenhower was firm: "[I]t certainly seemed to him about time for the British to allow us to try our hand," the NSC account of the meeting said.[25] And that same evening, at a meeting with British Foreign Secretary Anthony Eden, Eisenhower warned that the United States "might have to exercise a freer hand with relation to Iran and the oil situation."[26]

Nevertheless, in less than a month, three senior administration officials— Secretary Dulles, CIA Director Allen Dulles, and former CIA Director and then-Under Secretary of State Walter Bedell Smith—had maneuvered to establish an entirely new policy of working with the British to oust Mossadegh from power through a coup. They did so, according to the architect of the CIA coup plan, Iran specialist Donald Wilbur, merely because a new opportunity had apparently appeared: a prominent Iranian general had sounded out the U.S. Ambassador about supporting a coup he would initiate. Undersecretary Smith, according to Wilbur, "determined that the U.S. Government could no longer approve of the Mossadegh government and

24. Central Intelligence Agency, "Probable Developments in Iran Through 1953," NIE-75, January 9, 1953, Foreign Relations of the United States, 1952-1954, Iran, 1951-1954. https://history.state.gov/historicaldocuments/frus1951-54Iran/d152.

25. Memorandum of Discussion at the 135th Meeting of the National Security Council, March 4, 1953, document no. 171, Foreign Relations of the United States, 1952-1954, Iran, 1951-1954 (Washington, D.C.: U.S. Government Publishing Office, 2017). https://history.state.gov/historicaldocuments/frus1951-54Iran/d171.

26. Memorandum by the Secretary of State of a Meeting at the White House on the Evening of March 4, 1953, March 4, 1953, document no. 378, Foreign Relations of the United States, 1952-1954, Western Europe and Canada, Vol. VI, part 1. https://history.state.gov/historicaldocuments/frus1952-54v06p1/d378.

would prefer a successor government in which there would be no National Frontists"— referring to followers of Mossadegh's party.

The CIA's Near East Department was informed that it was authorized to "consider operations which would contribute to the fall of the Mossadegh government". Allen Dulles informed Kermit Roosevelt, the Director of Middle East operations, on April 4, 1953 that he would have $1 million immediately for the new program.[27] How the advocates of a coup prevailed on Eisenhower to sign off on a new policy toward Iran so sharply at odds with the premises of the March 4 NSC meeting has never been explained.

The CIA plan for a coup called for Iranian military forces to seize power against Mossadegh in the name of the Shah Mohamed Reza Pahlavi, the young monarch who had reigned ever since his father was deposed by allied occupation in 1941. The Shah would issue a decree naming Gen. Fazlullah Zahedi—the only major figure willing to openly oppose Mossadegh—as his Prime Minister. But the Zahedi plot quickly turned into a fiasco on August 17 when the Mossadegh government learned the details of the plan in advance from one of the participants and were waiting for Zahedi's military units to enter the city. Zahedi himself was forced to hide in the house of a U.S. diplomat.[28] The coup finally succeeded, not because of the power balance between the Mossadegh government and the forces of the U.S.-British clients, but because of the Agency's capabilities for deception and a serious mistake by Mossadegh himself.

Wilbur, the mastermind behind the plan, was a specialist on "black" and "grey" propaganda—spreading lies attributed either to the enemy or to a third party. Along with buying off a number of Majles members and other political groups with the help long-time British agents, the primary activity of the CIA team carrying out the coup plan was "grey" propaganda aimed at discrediting Mossadegh and the National Front. Wilbur himself, for example, forged documents appearing to show that Mossadegh himself was "anti-religious" and had "secretly collaborated" with the Tudeh—both blatant falsehoods.[29]

What was crucial to the success of the coup, however, was the deployment of a fake Tudeh Party crowd after the defeat of the original coup plan. Wilbur's redacted account clearly suggests—and five former CIA officers

---

27. Dr. Donald Wilber, "Overthrow of Premier Mossadeq of Iran, November 1952-August 1953," March 1954, National Security Archive Electronic Briefing Book No. 28, "The Secret CIA History of the Iran Coup," p. 2-3. https://nsarchive2.gwu.edu/NSAEBB/NSAEBB28/.

28. Abrahamian, *The Coup*, 185.

29. Abrahamian, *The Coup*, 178.

confirmed in interviews with historian Mark Gasiorowski—that the osten-
sibly Tudeh crowd that had carried out a violent rampage in Tehran that
included attacking the mausoleum of the Shah's father, Reza Shah, was in
fact organized by individuals paid by the Agency.[30] That CIA counterfeit
Tudeh crowd played a pivotal role in coup, because Mossadegh, respond-
ing to the demand from U.S. Ambassador Loy Henderson that he clear the
streets of all demonstrators, then ordered the Tudeh to keep its members off
the street. The Tudeh had obeyed Mossadegh's orders, apparently because
of its realization that the U.S. and British intelligence were deploying fake
Tudeh crowds for their own purposes. Those decisions had cleared the way for
another rampage by right-wing thugs—supplied by long-time British agents
who were part of the CIA's coup plot—which attacked National Front and
government targets and captured Mossadegh with the cooperation of military men from the coup group.[31] Mossadegh was tried for treason, served five
years in prison, then was put under house arrest until he died in 1956.

The Rise and Fall of the Shah

WITH THE ELIMINATION OF THE MOSSADEGH and the nationalist regime,
the Eisenhower administration lost no time in moving to eliminate
any vestige of the Tudeh Party in Iran, which it regarded as an obstacle to
consolidating the power of an anti-Communist U.S. client regime. A U.S.
Army Colonel was sent in September to help get the project started, and the
U.S. Embassy issued a justification for the it: "The notion that communism
feeds on suppression may be accepted to be communist inspired," it said.
"What they fear is firm police action." Within weeks, the new regime had

---

30. Wilbur, "Overthrow," 62-64; Mark Gasiorowski, "The 1953 Coup d'Etat in
Iran," International Journal of Middle East Studies, Vol. 19, no. 3, August 1987,
271-74 and fn. 66, 277.
31. Abrahamian, *The Coup*, pp. 185-194; Gasiorowski, "The 1953 Coup," Former
CIA officers told Gasiorowski that the CIA had penetrated the Tudeh Party at a
"very high level" and that the CIA's knowledge of the Party's orders to cadres was
therefore "very accurate". "The 1953 Coup," fn. 76, 277.

rounded up 1,200 members of the party, which grew to more than 3,000 by mid-1954.[32]

In 1957, the regime set up SAVAK, the Persian acronym for the National Organization for Security and Intelligence, which became the first police state in Iranian history, in which only groups loyal to the Shah could operate freely and any political dissent was vigorously repressed. SAVAK had 3,000 to 5,000 official personnel, but tens of thousands of informers throughout the society. The SAVAK earned a fearsome reputation for the use of torture and murder of dissidents. The CIA and Israel's Mossad took care of the training, and many SAVAK officers were sent to Israel for that purpose.[33]

The destruction by the Shah's regime of the secular nationalist and Marxist political forces cleared the way for the development of an Islamic political movement in Iran. That effect was first evident in the 1963, when demonstrations by Islamic followers of Ruhollah Khomeini against the Shah's regime occurred throughout Iran. The size of the protests—and the violent crackdown on them by government troops with live fire, killing an estimated 300 people—first established Khomeini's status as the leader of the movement against the Shah.[34]

Having crushed that Islamic uprising, the Shah proceeded to launch his "White Revolution"—a forced-draft campaign of Westernization and industrialization combined with an ambitious effort at semi-totalitarian political rule. The Shah's economic "revolution" was a grotesque imitation of Western capitalist industrialization telescoped into a single generation. The results outdid the early capitalist industrializing states in creating extremes of wealth and poverty. By 1972, Iran had one of the most unequal systems of income distribution in the entire world. The inequalities of income and living conditions were greatest in the Tehran and its environs, to which millions had been drawn from rural areas in search of work and lived in shantytowns without running water or other amenities. Meanwhile the Shah's rural "revolution" failed to benefit most of the rural population, as the government

---

32. Mark J. Gasiorowski, "Security Relations between the United States and Iran, 1953–1978," in Nikki R. Keddie and Mark J. Gasiorowsky, eds., Neither East Nor West: Iran, the United States and the Soviet Union (New Haven: Yale University Press, 1990), 148-151; Abrahamian, The Coup, 203.

33. Nikkie R. Keddie and Richard Yann, *Modern Iran: Roots and Results of Revolution* (New Haven: Yale University Press, 2006), p. 134.

34. Gary Sick, *All Fall Down* (New York: Penguin Books, 1985), pp 11-13; Stephen Kinzer, *All The Shah's Men: An American Coup and the Roots of Middle East Terror* (Hoboken, N. J.: John Wiley and Sons, 2003), pp. 76-80.

imposed artificially low prices on agricultural produce, impoverishing peas-ants to keep the urban middle class happy.[35]

The political effect of the new more extreme socio-economic inequalities was reinforced by the extreme corruption that allowed the Shah's family and senior officials to amass huge wealth. A January 1977 State Department intelligence report on the future of the Shah's regime observed that top mil-itary officials were "continuing to profit from their official positions," and that "only the most extreme are singled out for punishment." The Pahlavi Foundation, which held about $3 billion in the family's assets, had invest-ments in 207 companies, including the leading companies in the United States, and at the end of the Shah's reign the royal family's total wealth was estimated at $20 billion.[36]

Meanwhile, the Nixon administration responded in 1972 to the British military withdrawal from the Persian Gulf, the pressures for cutting military spending in the wake of U.S. setback in the Vietnam War, and the need to pull back from the U.S. military commitments in the Middle East, by mak-ing the Shah's Iran the U.S. regional surrogate for the entire Middle East. That decision was followed by a torrent of U.S. sales of its most sophisticated weapons systems to Iran, totaling more than $10 billion over the next five years. Along with a huge increase in its military budget, that made Iran the dominant military power in the region, with its largest navy and air force and the fifth-largest army in the world.[37]

But in late 1976, the unprecedented alliance between the Nixon adminis-tration and the Shah's regime suddenly came undone, because of conflicting U.S. and Iranian economic interests. The sums the Shah was spending on his national development and regional ambitions were beyond his means. He planned to raise the global price of oil by 20-25% at the next OPEC meeting on oil prices in January 1977 to cover his budget deficit. But the global econ-omy was already experiencing financial stress in 1976, and President Gerald Ford warned the Shah's emissary that the U.S. economy would fall back into recession with such a price increase and insisted on no increase in the oil

---

35. Ervand Abrahamian, *A History of Modern Iran* (Cambridge: Cambridge University Press, 2008), pp. 131-143.
36. Department of State, Bureau of Intelligence and Research, "The Future of Iran: Implications for the United States," Report no. 704, January 28, 1977. William Branigan, "Pahlavi Fortune: A Staggering Sum," Washington Post, January 17, 1979.
37. Sick, All Fall Down, pp. 14-17, 21; U.S. Military Sales to Iran: A Staff Report to the Subcommittee on Foreign Assistance of Committee on Foreign Relations, United States Senate, 94th Cong., 2nd Sess., July 1976 (Washington, D.C.: Government Printing Office, 1976), p. 5.

price by OPEC. The Saudis took advantage of the U.S.-Iranian conflict by volunteering a huge increase in its own production that flooded the market and undercut the Iranian effort to raise the global price.[38]

That OPEC meeting marked the end of the U.S. dependence on Iran as regional gendarme and began the unraveling of the Shah's regime. Inflation quickly soared to as high as 40 percent in 1977, while production plummeted by 50 percent, throwing millions of unskilled laborers out of work, most of whom were in Tehran. Historian Nikki Keddie observed that the economic crisis had "helped create a classic pre-revolutionary situation".[39]

As sociologist Theda Skocpol has pointed out, however, structural factors cannot explain the Iranian revolution, which was not driven by a party or movement of either the proletariat or the peasantry. Even if the economic conditions after 1976 were favorable to revolution, the organizing of revolt against the Shah's regime, as Skocpol writes, was "based on traditional centers of urban communal life and in networks of Islamic religious communication and leadership."[40]

The exiled Ayatollah Khomeini had already succeeded in transforming the political thinking of Iran's Shi'a clergy, turning them against the hereditary monarchy, which had been accepted for twelve centuries as the legitimate authority in Islamic society. Khomeini condemned it as a relic of polytheism and insisted that the overthrow of the Shah's monarchy was a religious duty.[41] Followers of Khomeini's political thinking became the main forces of the Iranian revolution, enabling it to overwhelm the might of the world's most powerful nation, in contrast to the ability of the U.S. and British governments to engineer the overthrow of the Mossadegh regime in 1953.

After a government editorial in January 1978 attacking Khomeini and the clergy as "black reactionaries", seminary students in Qom organized a march to the police station where they clashed with police. Two clerics were killed and dozens were wounded, and the clash began a cycle of protests and government repression that drew progressively more people into the movement. Nationwide demonstration spread across the country in February, as

---

38. Andrew Scott Cooper, "Showdown in Doha: The Secret Oil Deal that Helped Sink the Shah of Iran," *Middle East Journal*, vol, 62, no. 4, pp. 567-591.
39. Cooper, "Showdown," p. 590; Nikki R. Keddie, *Roots of Revolution: An Interpretative History of Modern Iran* (New Haven and London: Yale University Press,, 1981), 177.
40. Theda Skocpol, "Rentier State and Shi'a Islam in the Iranian Revolution," *Theory and Society*, Vol. 11, no 3 (November 1982), 270.
41. Abrahamian, *A History of Modern Iran*, 146-47.

rioters attacked symbols of western culture, including theaters, banks, bars, and even police stations.[42]

On September 8, 1978 the anti-Shah movement defied his order against street meetings, and as many as 500,000 protesters gathered in Tehran. When the crowd refused to disperse, commandoes fired on it indiscriminately, and 84 were killed. That was the first major blow to the pretensions of the United States to possess the power to keep the Shah on the throne. On November 9, the US Ambassador to Iran, William Sullivan, reported to the State Department in a cable entitled "Thinking the Unthinkable" that he did not believe the Shah could survive the demonstrations and that the Carter Administration should consider withdrawing support for the Shah and encouraging him to abdicate.[43]

But National security adviser Zbigniew Brzezinski, with the support of Secretary of Defense Harold Brown, still insisted on maintaining an absolute commitment to keeping the Shah in power. And when the Shah hesitated to use military force to against those demonstrations, State Department official Henry Precht recalled later, Brzezinski argued privately that the administration should urge the Shah to "send [his] troops out and shoot down as many people as necessary and bring an end to the rebellion once and for all."[44] Brzezinski and Brown represented the firmly-held belief of the national security state that the United States must use whatever means are necessary to hold on to an important U.S. position of power.

But the biggest blow to those U.S. pretensions of power was yet to come. The regime was planning to forbid demonstrations during the religious holiday of Ashura. But representatives of the Khomeini-led movement vowed to proceed with their plan for mass demonstration on that day in Tehran, and the government was forced to keep its troops away from site in Western Tehran. On December 11, the Islamic movement mounted a demonstration in which foreign embassies agreed more than two million participated calling for the return of Khomeini from exile and the establishment of an Islamic Republic.[45]

---

42. Jahangir Amuzegar, *Dynamics of the Iranian Revolution: The Pahlavis' Triumph and Tragedy* (Albany, State University Press of New York, 1991), 247-253

43. Cable from Sullivan to the State Department, "Thinking the Unthinkable," November 9, 1978, Document 30 in "The Carter Administration and the Arc of Crisis": Iran, Afghanistan and the Cold War in Southwest Asia, 1977-1981. https://www.wilsoncenter.org/sites/default/files/the_carter_administration_and_the_arc_of_crisis_1977-1981.pdf.

44. Henry Precht, "The Iranian Revolution 25 Years later: An Oral History with Henry Precht, Then State Department Desk Officer," *Middle East Journal*, 58 no. 1 (Winter 2004), 17.

45. Abrahamian, *A History of Modern Iran*, 159-161.

The Islamic opposition had dramatically demonstrated through that event the reality that, as one Western Ambassador put it, "[T]there already is an alternative government." The Shah's regime, he observed, "was powerless to preserve law and order on its own. It could do so only by standing aside and allowing the religious leaders to take charge."[46]

The Shah invited a figure from the opposition, Shahpur Bakhtiar, as prime minister and planned to remain in Iran long enough for Bakhtiar to establish himself. Bakhtiar, however, was immediately expelled from the opposition and denounced as a traitor. After Bakhtiar criticized Khomeini, saying that the Ayatollah intended to establish a theocracy, Khomeini called for his immediate overthrow. The Shah formally appointed Bakhtiar as Prime Minister on January 16, 1979 and later that same day, the Shah and his family left Iran for exile in Egypt, never to return.[47]

Khomeini returned from Paris on February 1 and appointed Mehdi Bazargan as Prime Minister. Now there were competing Prime Ministers, but armed partisans began attacking military bases, weapons factories, and government buildings. Khomeini supporters raided a weapons factory, capturing 50,000 machine guns and distributing them to supporters around Tehran. The city's martial law commander refused to use force against the Khomeini supporters and on February 11, the country's Supreme Military Council disbanded.[48]

The US maintained a diplomatic presence through all of this upheaval. But demonstrations in front of the US Embassy, actively encouraged by the clerical leadership, grew to the hundreds of thousands. After the Carter administration's decision to grant the Shah permission to enter the United States for treatment of cancer, on November 4, 1979, a group of pro-Khomeini university students stormed the embassy, took it over, and took all of the Americans inside hostage, beginning a 444-day standoff between Iran and the United States.

The students demanded the return of the Shah so that he could be tried and executed, but President Jimmy Carter called the hostages "victims of terrorism and anarchy." Millions of Iranians nevertheless celebrated the hostage-taking, remembering vividly how the CIA had destroyed the first truly independent Iranian government and put the Shah in power. For even the

---

46. R. W. Apple, "Reading Iran's Next Chapter," *New York Times*, December 13, 1978. https://www.nytimes.com/1978/12/13/archives/reading-irans-next-chapter-another-test-for-2-sides-expected-this.html.
47. Abbas Milani, *The Shah* (New York: St. Martins, 2011), 405-413.
48. Sepehr Zabir, *Iran Since the Revolution* (New York: Routledge, 2011, 17.

Carter Administration's decision to grant the Shah asylum so that he could seek treatment for cancer seemed like an act of imperialism.[49]

When negotiations with the new Iranian government failed to free the hostages, on April 24, 1980, Carter ordered the US military to attempt a rescue mission. But when only five of eight helicopters flown to a staging area in the Iranian desert arrived in operational condition, Carter ordered the mission to be aborted. During withdrawal, however, one of the helicopters crashed into a troop transport plane carrying both Delta Force operatives and jet fuel, killing eight soldiers and destroying both aircraft.

The hostages were finally released on January 20, 1981, simultaneously with Reagan's inauguration under an agreement negotiated in Algiers, but only after sensational television news coverage had generated popular hostility toward Iran for 13 months. It was only the beginning of a conflict that would ultimately bring the United States and the Islamic Republic of Iran to the brink of war.

49. James Buchan, *Days of God: The Revolution in Iran and Its Consequences.* (New York: Simon and Schuster, 2013), 257.

2. How Iran Became the Enemy

Unleashing Saddam's Chemical War

BEFORE ITS COLLAPSE, THE SHAH'S REGIME had been granted extraordinary power to protect U.S. regional interests at a time when the popular reaction to the Vietnam War had limited the national security state's freedom of action and forced a reduction in the military budget. Its replacement by an Islamic revolution that had a strong anti-imperialist ideology but that remained chaotic and militarily weak spurred the CIA to seek a way to reinstall the old regime without the Shah, who had died in mid-1980.

The Reagan administration's CIA Director William Casey explored that possibility and even identified the Shah's son Reza Pahlavi as a possible new head of state.[50] Nothing came of that Casey project, but the Iraqi invasion of Iran in late September 1980 and the subsequent development of the war quickly became the new administration's main preoccupation, especially when Iranian forces stopped the Iraqi advance in spring 1982 and began to go on the offensive.

The Reagan administration responded by deciding, as Reagan's National Security Council specialist on the Middle East, Howard Teicher, later recalled, that the administration did everything possible to prevent Iraq from losing the war with Iran. First it took Iraq off the list of state sponsors of terrorism states, so it would become eligible for certain U.S. export-promotion loans. More importantly, the CIA began sharing highly classified

---

50. Bob Woodward, *Veil: The Secret War of the CIA: 1981-1987* (New York: Pocket Books, 1987), 109-110.

intelligence on Iran's military assets and troop movements with the Iraqi high command.[51]

The most significant feature of that policy was that it flashed a green light for Saddam to carry out a chemical war against Iran that rivaled the infamous World War I chemical attacks and then provided international political-diplomatic cover for it. During summer 1983, the Reagan administration was well aware that Iraqi forces had been using chemical weapons against Iranian and Kurdish fighters in the border area almost daily.[52] The Iraqis attacked with mustard gas, the main chemical weapon used in World War I, which caused blisters not only in the throat and lungs but all over the body of the victim, and which had been outlawed by the adoption of the Geneva Protocol of 1925 outlawing such weapons in war.

The administration handed a demarche to the Iraqi Foreign Ministry expressing the administration's concern about chemical weapon, but it never put any real diplomatic pressure on Saddam's government over the issue. The reason was that, as the State Department's Iraq desk offer explained at the time, the U.S. did not want to "play into Iran's hands by fueling its propaganda against Iraq."[53]

The real U.S. policy was accurately reflected in special envoy Donald Rumsfeld's meeting with Saddam in December 1983. Rumsfeld—who carried with him a gift of a pair of golden spurs—agreed with Saddam on the need to reestablish diplomatic relations, which were broken by the United States in late December 1979, when Iran was put on the list of U.S. state sponsors of terrorism, and never brought up Iraq's use of chemical weapons.[54] The U.S. Embassy in Baghdad reopened in November 1984.[55]

Iraq's chemical war continued for five more years, climaxing with the use

---

51. Seymour Hersh, "U.S. Secretly Gave Aid to Iraq Early in its War against Iran," *New York Times*, January 26, 1992.

52. Department of State, Bureau of Politico-Military Affairs Information Memorandum from Jonathan T. Howe to George P. Shultz. "Iraq Use of Chemical Weapons," November 1, 1983, document 24, "Shaking Hands with Saddam Hussein: The U.S. Tilts toward Iraq, 1980-1984," National Security Archive Electronic Briefing Book No. 82, February 25, 2003. https://nsarchive2.gwu.edu/NSAEBB/NSAEBB82/#docs.

53. Joost R. Hiltermann, *A Poisonous Affair: America, Iraq and the Gassing of Halabja* (Cambridge: Cambridge University Press, 2007), 47-48

54. Hilterman, *A Poisonous Affair*, 46-51; William Arkin, "Why a War with Iraq is Inevitable," *Los Angeles Times*, September 15, 2002. Online at https://www.latimes.com/archives/la-xpm-2002-sep-15-op-arkin15-story.html.

55. Arkin, "Why a War with Iraq is Inevitable," *Los Angeles Times*, September 15 , 2002.

of both mustard gas and sarin nerve gas in four major offensives in 1988. The U.S. was complicit in that first use of deadly nerve gas in a war in human history, because Iraqi forces using the gas were heavily reliant on U.S. satellite imagery, maps, and other intelligence on Iranian troop movements, logistics facilities and Iranian air defenses, according to retired Air Force Col. Rick Francona, then the U.S. military attaché in Baghdad. "The Iraqis never told us that they intended to use nerve gas," Francona acknowledged in a 2013 interview. "They didn't have to. We already knew."[56]

The Iraqi Anfal campaign in early 1988 included an attack on the Kurdish town of Halabja near the Iran-Iraq border with sarin gas, killing 3,500 to 5,000—virtually all civilians—after it had been previously captured by Kurdish peshmerga troops supported by Iranian troops. When the United Nations actually investigated the Iraqi sarin attack on Halabja, the U.S. government came up with the false cover story that it believed Iran had also used chemical weapons in the town and sent it out to all U.S. Embassies for distribution to other governments in order to prevent a diplomatic crisis for Iraq over the atrocity.[57]

The human toll of the Iraqi use of mustard gas and sarin against Iranians was far greater than was widely known. Iranian specialists estimated that more than one million Iranian were exposed to the attacks, that 7,000 died immediately and 100,000 were severely injured, of which 55,000 still continued to suffer the agonizing after-effects decades later.[58] No American public figure ever raised moral objection to the U.S. role in the Iraqi use of those poison gases, which had been outlawed decades earlier. In contrast to that silence over Saddam's illicit use of sarin and when sarin was widely believed—but not proven—to have been used by Syrian government forces near Damascus in August 2013 and in Khan Sheikhoun in April 2014, U.S. national security and political elites demanded U.S. some military response, if not an all-out air offensive, against the Assad regime in retaliation.

56. Shane Harris and Matthew M. Aid, "Exclusive: CIA Files Prove America Helped Saddam as He Gassed Iran", Foreign Policy, August 26, 2013. Online at https://foreignpolicy.com/2013/08/26/exclusive-cia-files-prove-america-helped-saddam-as-he-gassed-iran/.
57. Hilterman, *A Poisonous Affair*, 126-127.
58. Scott Peterson, *Let the Swords Encircle Me* (New York: Simon and Schuster, 2010), 63.

Terrorism in Lebanon: Iranian, Israeli and American

O VER THE PAST FORTY YEARS, LARGE parts of the U.S. national security elite, including both CIA operations veterans and military officials, have maintained visceral hatred of Iran as a result of terrorist violence against Americans by Shiite allies of Iran in Lebanon and Kuwait in the early to mid-1980s. That deep and abiding U.S. military and CIA animus toward Iran and its Lebanese Hezbollah allies recalls not only the bombings of the U.S. Marine base near Beirut (which was part of an existing war in which U.S. Marines were intervening on behalf of one side in Lebanon's civil war), but the terror bombings of the U.S. Embassy in Beirut (which killed 32 Lebanese and 17 Americans, including 7 CIA officers and support personnel) and the U.S. Embassy in Kuwait; and the kidnapping, torture and killing of CIA Beirut station chief William Francis Buckley.

This narrative of Iranian-sponsored terrorism against Americans, which has influenced generations of officials ever since, focuses only on one side of a Lebanese conflict in which the use of murder and terrorism by U.S. allies was commonplace.[59] Before any of those bombings and kidnapping had been carried out, the CIA had already become deeply enmeshed in Lebanese sectarian violence and even terrorism. For years, it had been financing a paramilitary network under Bashir Gemayel, the leader of the Maronite Christian right-wing extremist Kateeb Party—also called the Phalange (the name of Spanish fascist dictator Francisco Franco's Party). He was a ruthless murderer who systematically eliminated his Christian rivals by assassination and massacre of their families. By 1982, the CIA had ended its relationship with Gemayel, whose murderous ways were regarded as too extreme.

But Gemayel had also become an asset of the Israelis, and ruthless Minister of Defense Ariel Sharon asked CIA Directory Casey in early 1982 to provide $10 million to support a paramilitary operation by Gemayel's group that would obvious be coordinated with the Israelis. The Israelis were promising to make him President of Lebanon in return for his full coopera-tion with Israeli plans after their invasion. Despite high-level concerns about

---

59. This account of the background to the dirty war between the CIA and its allies, on one side, and Iran's allies on the other is based on Bob Woodward, "Alliance with a Lebanese Leader"; *Washington Post*, September 29, 1987; George Shultz, Turmoil and Triumph: My Years as Secretary of State (New York: Scribner's, 1993), 65, 99-114, David Kennedy and Leslie Brunetta, "Lebanon and the Intelligence Community: A Case Study," CIA Library, May 8, 2007. https://www.cia.gov/library/center-for-the-study-of-intelligence/kent-csi/vol37no2/html/v37i2a05p_0001.htm

supporting one of the most unsavory figures in the entire Middle East, Casey agreed to the Israeli plan.

In August 1982, after the evacuation of PLO troops from Beirut, and the Israeli takeover, Gemayel became President of Lebanon with U.S. and Israeli backing. In mid-September Gemayal was killed by a massive bomb at his headquarters in Beirut. Two days later, the Israelis trucked Gemayel's killers to the Sabra and Shatilla Palestinian refugee camps in Beirut, where they massacred some 700 Palestinian civilians, including women and children— just as Sharon had planned from the beginning, telling U.S. envoy Philip Habib in August about "the need to clean out" those camps.

But the U.S. alliance with Israel drew it even more deeply into the maelstrom of terrorism in that country. Beginning in 1980 a group of senior Israeli military officers launched a campaign of terror bombings in areas of Lebanon where Palestinians congregated that killed hundreds of innocent civilians, using a fictitious right-wing Palestinian Christian organization the Israelis called the Front for the Liberation of Lebanon from Foreigners. One Israeli with knowledge of the campaign later commented, "We are speaking here of mass killings for killing's sake, to sow chaos and alarm, among civilians, too."[60] Many in Lebanon were sure the Israelis were behind the bombings.

All of these terrorist campaigns in Lebanon sponsored by the Israelis served to draw the United States into a sectarian war in which it was impossible for the U.S. government to avoid being identified with a sectarian government identified with Israeli-supported Phalangists. The marines had stumbled into a civil war between the Maronites and their Druze and Muslim foes. The terrorist bombings of U.S. embassies and the killing of Buckley carried out by Hezbollah were all terrorist actions, but they were also carried out in response to the series of Israeli-sponsored campaigns of terrorism.

Nor did the CIA forego is own terrorist revenge against Hezbollah. In 1984 CIA Director Casey arranged with the Saudis to assassinate Sheikh Fadlallah, the spiritual leader of Hezbollah. In the end, it was Lebanese intelligence who hired the hit men to the do the dirty work. The following March a car bomb plowed into the high rise building in Beirut where Fadlallah lived, killing 80 people and wounding 200 more, but Fadlallah was unhurt.[61]

Despite the fact that CIA and Israeli military terrorist bombings were,

---

60. Remi Brulin, "How the Israeli military censor killed a story about 'terrorist' bombing campaign in Lebanon in 1980s," Mondoweiss, October 23, 2019. https://mondoweiss.net/2019/10/it-is-time-to-break-the-silence-on-israeli-terrorist-campaign-in-lebanon-that-killed-100s/.
61. Bob Woodward, *Veil: The Secret Wars of the CIA* (New York: Pocket Books, 1987), 450-56.

if anything, on a wider scale than the terror bombings and killing of U.S. diplomatic and intelligence personnel in Lebanon and Kuwait in the early to mid-1980s, the U.S. national security elite continued to believe that its hostility toward Iran was justified in part by the actions of Shi'a militias under Iranian tutelage during that period.

Why the U.S. Refused to Make Peace with Iran

THE INITIAL RESPONSE OF THE GEORGE H. W. Bush administration to the end of the Iran-Iraq War was to entertain the possibility of improving relations with Iran, provided that Iran showed good will—especially on the problem of freeing U.S. hostages seized and held in Lebanon. Bush's January 1989 inaugural address suggested his willingness to make a reciprocal gesture if Iran was helpful in securing the release of the Americans hostages that had been taken by Shiite allies of Iran in Lebanon during the war. The administration's August 1991 "National Security Strategy" envisioned a possible thaw in relations provided Iran "makes clear it is lending no support to hostage-taking or other forms of terrorism."[62]

Iranian President Akbar Hashemi Rafsanjani responded positively to that opening, securing the release of the last American hostage in December 1991. Bush's national security adviser Brent Scowcroft told UN hostage negotiator Giandomenico Picco, who had dealt directly with Rafsanjani, that a reciprocal gesture was under consideration, such as taking Iran off the terrorist list, reducing economic sanctions or compensating Iran for the July 1988 U.S. navy shoot-down of the Iranian civilian airbus. But despite that gesture toward Washington, Scowcroft told Picco in April there would be no U.S. goodwill gesture after all.[63]

Resistance to any U.S. step toward rapprochement with Tehran from the new Director of the Central Intelligence Agency Robert M. Gates had surfaced immediately upon his taking over the agency in November 1991. Gates had told the Senate Armed Services Committee in January 1992 that Iran would "probably continue to promote terrorism" and that it had "embarked on an ambitious effort to develop its military and defense industries", including efforts to acquire weapons of mass destruction".

---

62. "National Security Strategy of the United States," August 1991.
63. Telephone interview with Giandomenico Picco by Gareth Porter, January 25, 2009, based on Picco's notes of a meeting with Scowcroft.

But Gates's view of Iran did not reflect the CIA National Intelligence Estimate (NIE) issued in late October. That estimate had concluded that Iran was "unlikely to conduct terrorism directly against U.S. or Western interests in the next two years", that its military forces were "less able to harm U.S. vital interests than they had been in the past" and that both President Rafsanjani and Supreme Leader Ali Khamenei believed Iran's interests lay in better relations with the West.[64]

Gates's hostility toward the opening to Iran was clearly related to the end of the Cold War and the Soviet Union itself, which posed a serious threat to the budgets of both the CIA and the Pentagon. As then-Chairman of the Joint Chiefs of Staff Gen. Colin L. Powell hinted in his introduction to the National Military Strategy published in January 1992, the Pentagon had an adversary problem with the end of the Soviet threat: "We can point to the North Korea, a weakened Iraq, and perhaps even a hostile Iran as specific threats for which we must maintain forces," wrote Powell.[65]

The need to find a way to make Iran seem more threatening explains why Gates was focusing on the threat of weapons of mass destruction and a new Iranian military buildup threat as keys to easing the transition from the old Soviet threat. In testimony before a joint session of House and Senate Intelligence Committees in April 1992, Gates highlighted "the rearmament of Iran" and argued that "proliferation is probably our highest priority".

But Gates was well aware from the CIA's own reporting and analysis that Iran was still woefully weak militarily and would be for many years to come. As one foreign diplomat in Tehran told the *New York Times* a few days after that testimony, Iran had to rebuild its military "almost from ground zero" after the devastating war with Iraq. And another diplomat said the estimated $2 billion a year Iran was spending on the military was "peanuts" compared to its minimum defense requirements.

The end of the Cold War also contributed to the new stage of hostility toward Iran from another angle. The State Department had previously put forward a rationale for negotiating with Iran to reduce tensions between the two antagonists: it could bring Iran into the regional diplomatic order as a balancer against Iraq. But the collapse of the Soviet Union and the new power balance in the Middle East had prompted Pentagon strategists to call for a more aggressive U.S. political-military posture in the region, as envisioned in the Pentagon policy guidance for FY1994-99 being drafted in 1991.

---

64. National Intelligence Estimate 34-91, "Iran under Rafsanjani: Seeking a New Role in the World Community?", October 1991, Online at https://www.cia.gov/library/readingroom/docs/DOC_0000602664.pdf.
65. National Military Strategy of the United States, January 1992, p. 3.

Iran as "Outlaw State"

THE IMPACT OF THE NEW UNIPOLAR power balance on Iran policy became even more pronounced in the early period of the Bill Clinton administration. That sharp swing in the national security bureaucracy toward a harder policy and propaganda line against the Islamic Republic was the result of both new bureaucratic interests in the Pentagon and the CIA as well as a new Israeli government policy of demonizing Iran that it also pressed on Washington.

Early in the new administration, a new bureaucratic focus on the threat of nuclear proliferation and on Iran as a future threat began to influence policymaking on Iran. In all the major national security institutions, officials were acquiring personal career and institutional interests in promoting one or both of those twin themes. The new Secretary of Defense, Les Aspin, concluded in his first major policy review that proliferation was "the new nuclear danger and it demanded new weapons and strategies for military operations to destroy such weapons.

The Joint Staff at the Pentagon began relying on a supposed Iran threat as part of the justification for U.S. military presence in the Middle East and beyond. In a document prepared for a Congressional briefing on "The Global Threat in the 1990s", the Joint Staff at the Pentagon portrayed a kind of Islamic version of the old Soviet-sponsored Communist revolutionary menace across the developing world. The "ultimate aim" of Iran, it said, was a "widespread, militant Islamic resurgence and the replacement of Western influence throughout a substantial part of the third world while dominating the Persian Gulf."[66]

But crucially important influence on the Clinton administration's Iran policy was the government of Israeli Prime Minister Yitzhak Rabin. Just three days after Clinton's election as President, Yossi Alpher, a top adviser to Rabin, warned, "Iran has to be identified as Enemy No. 1". And in London the following month, Rabin reportedly warned that Israel would face a threat of nuclear-tipped Iranian missiles within three to seven years.

Prior to Clinton's election, however, Rabin had not been worried about Iran as a threat to Israel. As late as August 1992, in fact, a newspaper columnist who had just met with Rabin quoted an unnamed senior official as

---

66. Joint Staff, "The Global Threat in the 1990s," May 1999, .unclassified document in files of Project on Government Oversight.

saying Israel faced "an existential threat that may materialize within seven to ten years *in light of Arab efforts to obtain nuclear weapons* [emphasis added]."[67]

Rabin's meeting with Clinton during the latter's presidential election campaign in October 1992 appears to have encouraged the Israeli Prime Minister to make a sharp turn in his own policy toward Iran. Clinton's Middle East policy adviser, Martin Indyk, did not reveal the substance of the Clinton-Rabin meeting in his memoirs, but he recalled that Clinton had told Indyk himself that a policy of "containment" of Iran was not "tough enough", and that the United States needed to "find a way to change their behavior or change the regime.[68]

So, Rabin almost certainly got the impression from that meeting that a Clinton administration would be taking a harder line toward Iran than the George H. W. Bush administration had. That revelation came just as Rabin had conceived his own political-diplomatic rationale for portraying Iran as an existential threat. Rabin had concluded that the time had come to negotiate directly with a weakened PLO, after the demise of the Soviet Union and the defeat and economic distress of its Iraqi patron. But he had a serious domestic political problem: such a Palestinian policy was very unpopular with the Israeli public. The only way he could see to justify it was to argue that it was necessary to strengthen Israel to deal with an even more dangerous approaching threat. The Rabin government presented the coming Iranian threat as "Islamic fundamentalism with nuclear arms behind them", as one Israeli analyst summarized it.[69]

The main Clinton administration policy shift on Iran, announced in May 1993, was to impose the same kind of harsh pressures on Iran as the U.S. was already imposing on the defeated Saddam Hussein regime in Iraq in what was to be called "dual containment". Because the policy had been developed by Indyk, an Australian citizen and former communications adviser to Israeli Prime Minister Yitzhak Shamir, without any input from the State Department Middle East Bureau or the intelligence community, it was "pretty much accepted" in Washington that the new policy had originated in Israel, according to the State Department Middle East policymaker at the time, Robert Pelletreau.[70]

---

67. Gareth Porter, "Israel's Construction of Iran as an Existential Threat," *Journal of Palestine Studies*, Vol 19, No. 1 (Autumn 2015), 45.
68. Martin Indyk, *Innocent Abroad: An Intimate Account of American Peace Diplomacy in the Middle East* (New York: Simon and Schuster, 2009), 16. 31.
69. Porter, "Israel's Construction," 46.
70. Trita Parsi, *Treacherous Alliance: The Secret Dealings of Israel, Iran and the U.S.* (New Haven: Yale University Press, 2007), 171.

After Indyk's initial presentation, Secretary of State Warren Christopher, who had already declared Iran to be an "international outlaw", vowed that Iran would be subject to U.S. and international isolation until it "halts its support for terrorism, curtails its military buildup, stops its subversion of other governments and ends its quest for nuclear weapons."[71]

The claims that Iran was carrying out or supporting terrorism and pursuing nuclear weapons and missiles to carry them, however, were false narratives serving to keep Iran "in the dock" of global opinion. The official U.S. conclusions on the two alleged cases of Iranian terrorism—the 1994 terror bombing of the Jewish community center in Buenos Aires and the 1996 bombing of a U.S. military facility in Saudi Arabia—were heavily distorted from the beginning by the U.S. desire to keep Iran in the dock of world opinion as an alleged state supporter of terrorism and were not supported by the actual evidence in either case.[72]

The Clinton administration's treatment of Iran as a combination terrorist state and Islamic extremist revolutionary force was also part of a broader policy of treating a large group of states as outlaws, which former Clinton NSC official Robert Litwak called a "demonization strategy". Litwak recalled that a Clinton administration official "conceded that unless the administration appeared 'completely maniacal' about Iran and other goes states," it couldn't get the G8 and its European and Japanese allies to take the desired actions against them. That problem accounts for much of the characterization of Iran's policies during that period, according to Litwak.[73]

The administration's posture toward Iran was clearly encouraged by the increased U.S. global and regional dominance as a result of both the collapse

---

71. Douglas Jehl, "U.S. Seeks Ways to Isolate Iran," *New York Times*, May 27, 1993. https://www.nytimes.com/1993/05/27/world/us-seeks-ways-to-isolate-iran-describes-leaders-as-dangerous.html.

72. On the Buenos Aires bombing, see Gareth Porter, "Bush's Iran/Argentina Terror Frame-Up," *The Nation*, February 4, 2008. https://www.thenation.com/article/bushs-iranargentina-terror-frame/;Mike Lasusa, "U.S. Involvement in the AMA Bombing Investigation: Keeping Iran 'In the Dock'," M.A. Thesis, American University, April 2016. https://auislandora.wrlc.org/islandora/object/researchpapers%3A3/datastream/PDF/view; Gabriel Levinas, La ley bajo los escombros: AMIA 20 anos de escubrimiento estatal [The Law under the Rubble: 20 Years of State Cover-up] (Buenos Aires:SudAmericana, 2014). On the Khobar Towers bombing, see Gareth Porter, "Who Bombed Khobar Towers? Anatomy of a Crooked Terrorism Investigation," Truthout, September 21, 2015. https://truthout.org/articles/who-bombed-khobar-towers-anatomy-of-a-crooked-terrorism-investigation/.

73. Robert Litwak, *Rogue States in U.S. Foreign Policy* (Washington, D.C.: Woodrow Wilson Center Press, 2000), 8-9.

of the Soviet Union and the new U.S. military presence in the Middle East after its 1992 victory over the Iraqi Army in Kuwait. The Clinton administration viewed itself as having responsibility for coercing all states who were not actively collaborating by "resocializing" them, as Litwak put it. But the power differential between the United States and Iran at that stage was so stark that it appeared to be a perfectly manageable task. In 1994, Clinton's national security adviser Tony Lake expressed complete confidence in achieving it, describing both Iraq and Iran as having "serious difficulties in challenging U.S. power."[74]

Cheney and the Neocons: Regime Change and War

THE GEORGE W. BUSH ADMINISTRATION'S LEADING policymakers believed the United States should use its newly-won global and regional power to eliminate regimes that refused to cooperate with the new U.S.-Israeli dominated regional order. That strategy, drafted by neoconservative Pentagon policymaker Douglas Faith after 9/11, called for the United States to target "regimes that support terrorism" and to "disrupt, damage or destroy" their military capabilities, thus paving the way for regime change. The main targets of the strategy were the Saddam Hussein regime in Iraq, the Assad regime in Syria and the biggest prize of all: the Islamic Republic of Iran. After speaking at a public even in 2008, however, Faith himself revealed that the list of states to be taken down under the strategy included Iraq, Iran, Syria, Libya, Sudan and Somalia.[75]

Iran was understood as the final stage of the process, to be achieved once the U.S. military had established firm control over Iraq. Bush's national security adviser Condoleezza Rice supported working covertly on that objective. Rice didn't agree, however, to the neoconservative demand that the administration declare it publicly as a policy objective, according to Hillary Mann Leverett, who was the coordinator for the Persian Gulf and Afghanistan on the NSC staff.

---

74. Tony Lake, "Confronting Backlash States," *Foreign Affairs*, March/April 1994, 48, 55.

75. Douglas Feith, *War and Decision: Inside the Pentagon at the Dawn of the War on Terrorism* (New York: Harper, 2009), pp. 81-85; Gareth Porter, "Pentagon Targeted Iran for Regime Change after 9/11", Inter Press Service, May 5, 2008. http://www.ipsnews.net/2008/05/politics-us-pentagon-targeted-iran-for-regime-change-after-9-11/.

Nevertheless, Rice, a Soviet specialist by training, believed that President Mohamed Khatemi, elected in the 2005 Iranian presidential election, was the "Gorbachev" of the Islamic regime, who sought reform without bringing down the system. She figured, therefore, that the U.S. problem was to find and support the Iranian "Yeltsin" who would support declaring a secular state.[76]

Rice never found her Iranian Yeltsin, but it didn't matter, because Cheney was determined to attack Iran in any case. It was clear even to Cheney by late 2006 that the neoconservative aim of gaining military and political control over Iraq was a pipe dream, so he and his staff decided that it was time to turn to military force. Cheney had long viewed the charge that Iran had carried out a secret nuclear weapons program from 2001 to 2003 as a justification for a major attack on Iranian military assets. But in late 2006, the idea had been presented to the Joint Chiefs of Staff, and they had rejected it.

Another option Cheney's staff was keen on was to hit Syrian military targets, in the hope that it might "rattle" the Assad regime sufficiently to end his close relationship with Iran. Cheney's Middle East adviser, David Wurmser, had long been convinced that if the Syrian regime could be brought down, it would destabilize the Islamic Republic. When Israeli Prime Minister Ehud Olmert asked President George W. Bush to bomb an alleged nuclear reactor being built by North Koreans in the Syrian desert in Spring 2007, Cheney pushed hard for U.S. military strikes not only on that target but Hezbollah weapons storage sites in Syria, according to then-Defense Secretary Robert M. Gates's account. But Cheney was the only Bush adviser arguing for U.S. military intervention in Syria, and Bush rejected the option. The Israeli Air Force then went ahead and bombed the mysterious building itself. Cheney's final effort to get a strike against Iran was a proposal in mid-2007 for U.S. military retaliation for a future incident in Iraq in which U.S. combat deaths could be blamed on Iran. Cheney was hoping to exploit a dubious propaganda theme that the U.S. command in Iraq had begun pushing in 2007 that Iran was providing armor-penetrating roadside bombs to Shiite militias in Iraq that were killing U.S. troops. He proposed an airstrike on an Iranian Islamic Revolutionary Guard base if the U.S. could find evidence for Iranian responsibility for any such attack. But Gates and the Pentagon again scuttled the idea, demanding to know how U.S.-Iranian escalation would unfold

---

76. Gareth Porter interview with Hillary Mann Leverett, McLean, Virginia, March 14, 2013.

after such an attack, according to former State Department official J. Scott Carpenter. Cheney and his staff were unable to answer the question.[77]

Thus, the neoconservative idea of using U.S. might to force regime change in Iran ended with a whimper in 2007. That fact should have raised serious questions about the ability of the United States to coerce Iran on issues of central importance to the Iran state. But the administration had already spent years imposing the 2006 United Nations Security Council resolution forbidding Iran from any enrichment of uranium—and levying sanctions against Iranian institutions and individuals for refusing to comply with it.

Those UN resolutions and sanctions firmly established the idea that the United States could force Iran to comply with U.S. policy demands, regardless of the actual circumstances, by using it global diplomatic and economic power. They set the stage for both the Obama administration's campaign of coercive diplomacy and the Trump administration's bravado in tearing up the nuclear agreement that had been so painfully negotiated and demanding Iranian concessions so extreme that they could only be a cover for a de facto regime change policy.

---

77. Gareth Porter, "Pentagon halted Cheney ploy to start war with Iran - ex-diplomat," *The Daily Star* (Beirut), June 9, 2008. http://www1.dailystar.com.lb/News/Middle-East/2008/Jun-09/79919-pentagon-halted-cheney-ploy-to-start-war-with-iran-ex-diplomat.ashx.

3. Creating a False Iran Nuclear Narrative

FOR NEARLY THREE DECADES, OVER FIVE different administrations, U.S. Iran policy has been enveloped in a political narrative that portrayed the Islamic Republic as secretly working on the ultimate goal of obtaining nuclear weapons. The narrative has woven a fictional account of Iranian policy while completely eliminating from the story the aggressive role the U.S. played in pressuring Iran to give up its sovereign right to a peaceful nuclear program.

This false narrative is not simply a problem of the deliberate construction of false history—although some of that has certainly happened. It is also a matter of U.S. intelligence going off the rails from the beginning and producing a picture of Iranian policy that was increasingly warped as time went on and a media system that never once questioned what was served up by U.S. officials.

The Real Origins of Iran's Enrichment Program

THE MOST CRUCIAL ELEMENT OF THIS false narrative is its presentation of the original Iranian decision in the mid-1980s to seek the technology for enriching uranium on the international black market as evidence of a nuclear weapons ambition. In fact, Iran had intended in reviving the nuclear program started by the Shah to rely on a French-owned consortium to supply the fuel for its lone nuclear reactor at Bushehr. The decision to obtain enrichment technology was a response to a Reagan administration decision in 1984 to pressure European allies to end all nuclear cooperation with Iran. As a result, France terminated its previous arrangement with Iran to provide the fuel for Bushehr, Iran's only nuclear reactor, which it inherited from the Shah's regime.[78]

The U.S. pursued that policy of denial of any foreign assistance, moreover, despite its own admission that it had no evidence that the Bushehr reactor presented any proliferation risk, or that Iran had violated its obligations under the under the Non-Proliferation Treaty (NPT). That made the U.S. policy a blatant violation of the NPT, which guarantees all signatory states access to such technology for "peaceful purposes". And the policy was adopted as part of the U.S. stance of supporting Iraq in the Iran-Iraq War. "It was part of the Iran-Iraq War syndrome," Reagan's NSC director for Near East and South Asia Geoffrey Kemp acknowledged in a 2013 interview.[79]

Iranian national pride and insistence on its full national rights ruled out bowing to the U.S. pressure and giving up its a peaceful nuclear program under the NPT. Iran's decision to find the enrichment technology on the black market should not have been a surprise to U.S. policymakers. But it is clear that no thought was given to the harshly unjust and provocative character of the U.S. policy. And after the U.S. government learned about the Iranian decision to obtain that technology, it began to accuse Iran of pursuing nuclear weapons.

When the IAEA first reported the details of Iran's conversion and enrichment programs in the over the years, the news media published sensational stories on a variant of the theme of Iran's "hiding a vast clandestine nuclear effort for 18 years," as the *Christian Science Monitor* story put it.[80] Those stories served to establish the official U.S. narrative of Iran as a would-be nuclear weapons state firmly in the public consciousness.

Much of the press coverage conveyed the impression that Iran had been carrying out uranium enrichment for all those years. But in reality, Iran had not even tested a single centrifuge with uranium until 1999 and didn't feed nuclear material into more than one machine until 2002. Contrary to the

---

78. The original Iranian nuclear program of the early 1980s and the U.S. policy of pressuring the Europeans to refuse to cooperate with it is described in Gareth Porter, *Manufactured Crisis: The Untold Story of the Iran Nuclear Scare* (Charlottesville, Va: Just World Books, 24-32.

79. Gareth Porter interview with Geoffrey Kemp, July 18, 2013.

80. Scott Peterson, "Evidence of Possible Work on Nukes Tests Iran's Credibility," *Christian Science Monitor*, February 26, 2004, 7.

popular impression created by the media, it had taken Iran nearly 18 years merely to acquire the necessary technology to begin the process of enriching uranium.

There was also a logical explanation other than work on a nuclear weapon for Iran's decision not to inform the IAEA about its purchases of technology or about some of its tests. Any reporting about where it purchased the technology would have resulted in U.S. and allied governments shutting down those channels. And Iranian small-scale experiments on uranium conversion with the uranium purchased secretly from China in the 1990s took place during a period in which Iran was also negotiating with China on the provision of a uranium conversion facility. So, any such reporting of those experiments would have led quickly to the revelation of China as the source of the uranium and would have unleashed strong U.S. diplomatic pressure on China to cease all nuclear cooperation with Iran.[81]

By erasing the real story of Iran's decision to obtain its own capability for uranium enrichment, the falsified narrative encouraged the creation of fabrications aimed at reinforcing it. The most widely published such fabrication is a purported "intelligence report" from an unnamed intelligence service supposedly providing the gist of a meeting between President Ali Khamenei and top political and security officials in April 1984. According to the report, Supreme Leader Khomeini had "decided to reactivate the nuclear program" in order to serve as a "deterrent in the hands of God's soldiers" and to "prepare [Iran] for the emergence of the Imam Mehdi".[82]

But that story, which was said to have been included in a draft report prepared by the International Atomic Energy Agency (IAEA) staff on evidence of Iran's covert nuclear weapons work, is easily identifiable as a crude fabrication. It is well documented that the Iranian government had made the decision to restore an active nuclear program in 1982—two years before the alleged meeting. And it was well known that Khomeini had regarded the

---

81. On the misleading press coverage of IAEA revelations about the 18-year Iranian enrichment program and the reasons for Iranian secrecy about some of the tests, see Porter, *Manufactured Crisis*, 46-51, 54-58.

82. "Internal IAEA Information Links the Supreme Leader to 1984 Decision to Seek a Nuclear Arsenal" ISIS Repots, Institute for Science and International Security April 20, 2012.

idea of the return of the Muslim messiah, the Mehdi that is advocated by some fundamentalist Shi'a, as dangerous nonsense.[83]

Why Iran Never Produced Weapons of Mass Destruction

OFFICIAL AND MEDIA ACCOUNTS OF IRAN's nuclear program have studiously avoided the most important evidence bearing on Iran's policy toward nuclear weapons: the story of how and why Iran failed to use chemical weapons against Iraq during the Iran-Iraq War.

The official U.S. position through the early 2000s was to simply deny that fact. A 1990 Defense Intelligence Agency report claiming that Iran had used cyanide in the Kurdish town of Halabja, which had been gassed by Iraqi troops. But Patrick Tyler, who had written a story based on that DIA report for the *Washington Post*, later learned that its authors had been involved in a DIA program that provided the Iraqi Air Force with detailed intelligence on Iranian military targets, including Tehran and other cities. Tyler concluded that the claim that Iranian had used poison gas had no credibility.[84]

But Iran was perfectly capable of producing a chemical weapon, and in fact it went all the up to the final stage of weaponization before the end of that war. The real reason that Iran did not use chemical weapons in retaliation against Iraq's expensive gas attacks against Iran is that it was forbidden from doing so by the Supreme Leader Ayatollah Khomeini on grounds of Islamic law. Khomeini's decision amounted to a fatwa—a judgment on

---

83. On the restart of the Iranian nuclear programs in 1982, see David Patrikarakos, *Nuclear Iran: The Birth of an Atomic State* (London: L. B. Tauris, 2012), 103-104. On Khomeini's disdain for the cult of the return of the Mehdi, see Yossi Melman an Meir Javadanfar, *The Nuclear Sphinx of Tehran* (New York: Carroll an GRAF, 2007), 45; Babak Sarfarez, "The Hidden Imam and His Cult," Tehran Bureau, July 25, 2010. https://www.pbs.org/wgbh/pages/frontline/tehranbureau/2010/07/mahdi-slideshow.html. For major news outlet reports that accepted the fabricated story unquestioningly, see James Risen, "Seeking Nuclear Insight in Fog of the Ayatollah's Utterances," *New York Times*, April 13, 2012; Joby Warrick, "Iran's Supreme Leader Embraced Concept of Nuclear Arms, Archived Document Suggests," Washington Post, April 20, 2012.

84. Patrick Tyler, *A World of Trouble: The White House and the Middle East-from the Cold War to the War on Terror* (New York: Farrar, Straus and Giroux, 2008), pp. 336-38; Gareth Porter interview with Patrick Tyler, May 17, 2013.

Islamic law by a qualified Islamic scholar—and because of Khomeini's role as the "guardian jurist" in the Shi'a Islamic system of "Guardianship of the Islamic Jurist" (*Velayat-e Faqih*), his fatwa had the force of law for the entire Iranian government.[85]

Khomeini's ban on producing chemical weapons or any other weapons of mass destruction was recounted by the chief of Iran's wartime Ministry of Military Supply Mohsen Rafighdoost in Tehran in 2014.[86] Rafighdoost, who had been a senior Islamic Revolutionary Guard Corps Official, recalled that a dramatic increase in Iraqi gas attacks on Iranian troops in southern Iraq, using both mustard gas and the nerve gas Tabun, had prompted him to create new groups of specialists in the ministry to work on chemical, biological and nuclear weapons. He then met with Khomeini, hoping to get his approval for the new initiative, including the group's plan to work on nuclear weapons.

But in a meeting with Rafighdoost, Khomeini ruled out the production of any weapons of mass destruction as illicit under Islam. "Imam told me that, instead of producing chemical weapons, we should produce defensive protection for our troops," Rafighdoost recalled. Khomeini further told him, "We don't want to produce nuclear weapons" and instructed him to send the scientists to Iran's civilian Atomic Energy Organization.

In June 1987, Iraqi aircraft bombed residential areas of the ethnic Kurdish city of Sardasht with mustard gas canisters, exposing 8,000 residents and killing hundreds of civilians. Rafighdoost recalled that he then began working with the defense ministry to procure the chemical precursors for mustard gas and to manufacture the chemicals necessary for such a weapon but did not weaponize them.

Then he met again with Khomeini in late 1987, hoping to get his approval for weaponizing the mustard gas. Rafighdoost told him what he had already been done and asked his view on "this capacity to retaliate". But again, Khomeini firmly rejected his request. "It is *haram* [forbidden] to produce such weapons," he said. Then Khomeini asked him, "If we produce chemical weapons what is the difference between me and Saddam?" He also reiterated his ban on nuclear weapons, saying "Don't talk about nuclear weapons at all."

In February 1988, Saddam stepped up missile attacks on Iranian cities and threatened to load the missiles with chemicals. One-third to one-half of

---

85. For an explanation and brief history of the concept of Velayat-e Faqih and its role in the government of the Islamic Republic from its inception in 1979, see Flynt Leveret and Hillary Mann Leveret, *Going to Tehran* (New York: Metropolitan Books, 2013), 172-73, 176-182.

86. Gareth Porter, "When the Ayatollah Said No to Nukes," *Foreign Policy*, October 15, 2014. https://foreignpolicy.com/2014/10/16/when-the-ayatollah-said-no-to-nukes/.

the population of Tehran evacuated in a panic. Without chemical weapons of its own, however, it was all but impossible for Khomeini to continue the war. When Iranian forces began announcing the "bitter decision" to accept the ceasefire with Iraq in August 1988, Khomeini said he did it "in light of the enemy's use of chemical weapons and our lack of equipment to neutralize them."[87]

No one has ever offered any explanation other than Khomeini's Islamic fatwa against all weapons of mass destruction for Iran's failure to use chemical weapons against Iraq. But the Iranian Supreme Leader's refusal to allow the use weapons of mass destruction on religious grounds—even though the consequences of were extremely costly to Iran's own military and civilian population—still remains unacknowledged in the official and media narrative.

Many Islamic Revolutionary Guard Corps (IRGC) officials like Rafighdoost and others involved in defense issues undoubtedly hoped that, after Khomeini's death in 1989, his successor, Ayatollah Ali Khamenei, would reverse Khomeini's absolute prohibition on possession of WMDs for deterrence purposes. But Khamenei instead issued his own fatwa against possession of nuclear weapons in the mid-1990s in the form of a letter to an official who had asked his religious opinion on nuclear weapons. The letter was not released to the public, however, according to Hossein Mousavian, then head of the Foreign Relations Committee of the Supreme National Security Council (SNSC).[88]

Khamenei may have hesitated to make his anti-nuclear fatwa public in the mid-1990s, because some senior officials were arguing for a degree of ambiguity to allow Iran to take full advantage of the "latent deterrent" value of its uranium enrichment program. A decade later, influential figures went public with that idea, supporting a policy that emulated the "Japan model" of nuclear policy—remaining a non-nuclear weapons state but letting potential foes know that the capability existed.[89]

In late 1990s some figures in IRGC military research institutions went further, arguing that they should be able to acquire the knowledge of how to build a nuclear weapon, even if producing such a weapon remained forbidden. And some specialists even began research projects on nuclear weapons on their own, without the approval of Khamenei, as a senior official involved

---

87. Porter, "When the Ayatollah Said No to Nukes".
88. Porter, "When the Ayatollah Said No to Nukes".
89. Porter, *Manufactured Crisis*, 75-77.

in the issue acknowledged to French Ambassador Francois Nicoulaud in October 2003.[90]

But in March 2003, after the construction of Iran's enrichment facility had been revealed, Khamenei invoked religious grounds for opposing nuclear weapons, saying, "We are not interested in an atomic bomb. We are opposed to chemical weapons....These things are against our principles." And in August, he even effectively made public his own fatwa, and linked it to Khomeini's wartime ban. "[B]y principle and fundamentals, we are against weapons of mass destruction," he declared, "just like we have considered biological and chemical weapons as prohibited weapons even at the time of the Imposed War [i.e., the Iran-Iraq War]."

In October 2003, at the same time that SNSC Secretary Hassan Rouhani moved quickly to reach agreement with the UK, France and Germany on a voluntary cessation of enrichment work, he sent a circular to all departments and agencies requiring a complete report on any work, past or present, related to the nuclear issue. The following week, Hossein Shariatmadari, editor of the conservative newspaper Kayhan and a close political ally of Khamenei, told Robert Collier of the *San Francisco Chronicle* that Khamenei had forced those who were still working on their own nuclear weapons-related research to "admit that it is forbidden under Islam."[91]

Four years later U.S. intelligence acquired some personal communication in which Iranian researchers had complained that their projects had been shut down in 2003.[92] But the inference that those researchers had been working on a government-approved nuclear weapons program was a reflection of the strong commitment of the CIA's own weapons analysts to that belief rather than the strength of the evidence. In light of the details now available of the IRGC's preparatory work on a chemical weapon program without Khomeini's approval, it is far more likely that IRGC researchers had done preliminary studies on nuclear weapons in the hope that Khamenei would change his mind about his earlier fatwa.

---

90. Personal communication to Gareth Porter from Ambassador Francois Nicoullaud, July 28, 2013.

91. Robert Collier, "Nuclear Weapons Unholy, Iran Says," *San Francisco Chronicle*, October 31, 2003. https://www.sfgate.com/news/article/Nuclear-weapons-unholy-Iran-says-Islam-forbids-2580018.php.

92. Greg MIller, "New Data Set Off a Series of Recalculations by the U.S. Intelligence Community," *Los Angeles Times*, December 5, 2007; Dafna Linzer, "Diving Deep, Unearthing a Surprise," *Washington Post*, December 8, 2007.

How the CIA Got Iran's Nuclear Program Wrong

THE CIA'S FAILURE TO REJECT THE Bush administration's shady case for invading Iraq based on alleged WMDs is generally accepted as an egregious case of intelligence analysis warped by political pressure from policymakers. But the record of CIA analysis on Iran's nuclear program has been even worse by any reasonable reckoning—and it has gone on for decades. The debacle of U.S. intelligence on Iran's nuclear program is the result of a policy climate regarding Iran in which analysts understand that they are expected to find evidence that supports the suspicion that Iran aims at having nuclear weapons.[93]

The creation of such a climate began in late 1990, when the George H. W. Bush administration initiated a series of meetings with the other members of the "Nuclear Suppliers Group"—the states that exported nuclear technology—to persuade them not to sell to Iran, on the grounds that, as one unnamed State Department official told the *Los Angeles Times*, Iranian scientists were "conducting research on enrichment and reprocessing for nuclear weapons".

Then, in September 1991, CIA Director Robert M. Gates set up a new "Nonproliferation Center" at the agency, staffed mainly with technical experts on WMDs from CIA but supplemented with specialists from other agencies. The center's specialists were strong on tracking commercial sources of WMD-related technology and other such technical matters that served Pentagon needs, but had no knowledge of the target countries' politics, policies or history, according to three former senior intelligence analysts who had worked with those specialists on analytic products in the early 1990s. That technical bent created a natural tendency to assume that target countries were involved in proliferation.[94]

That was the policy and institutional setting in which U.S. and allied intelligence agencies began intercepting telex messages between Iran and companies selling nuclear and dual-use technology in the early 1990s. The

---

93. Tadeusz Strulak, "The Suppliers Group," Non-Proliferation Review (Fall 1993), 3; Jim Mann, "Iran's Nuclear Plans Worry U.S. Officials," *Los Angeles Times*, January 27, 1991.

94. Interviews with former senior intelligence analysts familiar with the Center's approach to proliferation issues in the 1990s, including former director of the State Department's Bureau of Intelligence and Research Thomas Fingar and former CIA intelligence officer for the Near East and South Asia Ellen Laipson. See Porter, Manufactured Crisis, 219-222.

messages, which often mentioned Sharif University, included orders for rings magnets, fluoride and fluoride-handling equipment, vacuum equipment and other technologies, all of which could be used in a centrifuge uranium enrichment program but could also have been for non-nuclear applications.

What excited the intelligence analysts, however, was that the telexes bore the telex number of the Physics Research Center, which had done work for Iran's Defense Ministry in the past. They cited the telexes as evidence of a military-run—and therefore nuclear weapons-related—nuclear program, although that was not the only possible explanation. Based on the analysts' judgment, administration officials referred in 1992 to a "suspicious procurement pattern" as the basis for its diplomatic interventions to prevent Argentina and China from providing research reactors to Iran.[95]

The intelligence community did not offer any intelligence estimate suggesting that Iran was undertaking a nuclear weapons program, however, or carry out any official assessment of Iran's nuclear intentions until 2001. The drafting of the new estimate was under the firm control of a new CIA Weapons Intelligence, Nonproliferation, and Arms Control Center created earlier that year out of the old NPC. That meant that it was even more heavily dominated by the technical specialists, who tended to assume that any indication of the technical capability to produce nuclear weapons was evidence of intent, as Paul Pillar, who participated in the process as CIA National Intelligence Officer for Near East, observed. Pillar recalled that no hard evidence of a nuclear weapons work had been obtained by U.S. Intelligence. "We're talking about things that are a matter of inference, not direct evidence," said Pillar.[96]

Furthermore there is documented evidence of a successful effort by the CIA Operations Department, supported by then-CIA Director George Tenet, to suppress hard intelligence evidence that Iran was not planning to obtaining nuclear weapons in order to ensure that the new NIE would reach the conclusion desired by Vice-President Dick Cheney that Iran was secretly working on nuclear weapons. A CIA operative obtained a report from what the CIA considered to be a "highly valued source" in Iran in 2001 that Iran had no intention of "weaponizing" the uranium it was planning to enrich. However, James L. Pavitt, Deputy CIA Director for Operations, who

95. Herbert Krosney, *Deadly Business: Legal Deals and Outlaw Weapons* (New York Four Walls Eight Windows, 1993), 263-65; Steve Coll, "U.S. Halted Nuclear Bid by Iran," *Washington Post*, November 17, 1982. https://www.washingtonpost.com/archive/politics/1992/11/17/us-halted-nuclear-bid-by-iran/0e215f24-43b2-4791-b24a-ea23b46b5a28/.

96. Interviews with Paul Pillar by Gareth Porter, July 25, 2012 and April 26, 2013.

controlled the flow of intelligence reporting on the Iran nuclear issue to CIA analysts, ordered the operative not to circulate any report on the information and to have no further contact with the source. The analysts working on Iran, including Pillar as the National Intelligence Officer for the Middle East, were never given access to that report.

Apart from the determination of Cheney to have intelligence supporting his hard line toward Iran, Pavitt had a personal motive for that intervention: he had pushed for the covert operation "Project Merlin" carried out in early 2000 to get Iran to bite on a phony design for a nuclear weapon, based on the still unconfirmed suspicion that Iran wanted nuclear weapons. He didn't want an NIE that could cast doubt on the rationale for that operation.[97]

The 2001 NIE delivered the judgment that Cheney and Pavitt had desired. It bore the title, "Iran Nuclear Weapons Program: Multifaceted and Poised to Succeed, but When?"[98]

The original analysts' inferences from the telexes had remained the main basis for that assessment. But when Iran finally explained those telexes to the IAEA in late 2007 and early 2008, it became clear that the intelligence analysts working on the Iran nuclear issue had been wrong all along: an IAEA report in February 2008 detailing the voluminous documentation provided by Iran showed that the former head of the Physics Research Center, Sayyed Abbas Shahmoradi-Zavareh, who had been simultaneously a professor at Sharif University, had procured the dual use items in question for various academic departments of Sharif University at the request of the departments themselves. The Iranian documentation was so complete and overwhelming in its detail that, after investigating on the ground at Sharif University, the IAEA was forced to acknowledge that what it had found "was not inconsistent with the stated use of the equipment."[99]

---

97. The whole episode involving the suppression of the most important intelligence on Iran's intentions up to that point is recounted in Gareth Porter, "How 'Operation Merlin' Poisoned U.S. Intelligence on Iran," *Consortium News*, March 3, 2018. https://consortiumnews.com/2018/03/03/how-operation-merlin-has-poisoned-u-s-intelligence-on-iran/

98. Paul K. Kerr, *Iran's Nuclear Program: Status*, Congressional Research Service, September 19, 2009, 16, fn. 86.

99. IAEA report GOV/4/2008, February 22, 2008, 3-4. https://www.iaea.org/sites/default/files/gov2008-4.pdf.

Fabricated Documents that Changed World Politics

A CRUCIAL TURNING POINT IN THE POLITICS of the Iran nuclear issue was the CIA's acquisition in mid-2004 of a large collection of documents said to have been from inside an alleged Iranian covert relearn program from 2001 to 2003. Their origin remained shrouded in mystery for years. The story that was leaked to the *New York Times* identified the source as an Iranian engineer or scientist who was a participant who had been recruited to spy on the program. The source's wife was said to have managed to smuggle the documents he had collected out of Iran on his laptop—thus the collection was sometimes called the "laptop documents".[100]

Those documents ultimately became the evidentiary basis on which the United States and its allies accused Iran of a covert nuclear weapons program, threatened war against Iran and asked its European allies, and got Russia and China to agree to agree impose United Nations Security Council Sanctions against Iran, which ultimately led to a Security Council resolution demanding that Iran cease all enrichment activities.

The documents that had the biggest political-diplomatic impact were a series of technical drawings showing the Shahab-3 Iranian ballistic missile with a nuclear weapon in the warhead. Another document showed a bench-scale system for conversion of uranium for enrichment. Analysts raised serious questions about these two studies from the beginning, however, because both had serious technical errors. The errors in the conversion system were so obvious that the head of the IAEA Safeguards Department acknowledged in an official briefing on the papers that it had "technical inconsistencies".

But the documents showed even more fundamental signs of having been fabricated: inconsistencies between those studies and the well-documented history of Iranian nuclear and missile programs. The missile shown in the schematic drawings was the original Shahab-3 missile with warhead in the shape of "dunce cap". But Iran had discovered that that missile was problematic: it failed in two of its first three tests, and its range was too limited to reach more than a small fraction of Israeli territory. So, it couldn't serve as an effective deterrent to U.S. and Israeli attack. In mid-2004, Iran tested for the first time the new, redesigned model of the missile that would increase

---

100. This account of the "laptop documents" is drawn from a much more detailed account and analysis in Porter, *Manufactured Crisis*, 191-216.

its the range from as little as 800 miles to 1,000 miles. That new model had a warhead with a "triconic" or "baby bottle" shape.[101]

The decision to design a new, improved model of the Shahab-3 missile had been announced by Iran's Defense Ministry in 2000, according to Congressional testimony by the CIA's intelligence officer for strategic and nuclear programs, Robert Walpole. But the earliest date for laptop documents showing the drawings of the missile was August 28, 2002. Obviously, it would have made no sense for a top-secret Iranian nuclear weapons research program to be doing technical drawings of how to mate a nuclear weapon with the old version of a missile that had been abandoned. But outside intelligence agencies had no idea what the new version looked like until mid-2004, which would explain why the fabricated documents showed the warhead of a missile that had been abandoned by the time the alleged covert nuclear weapons program was supposedly started.[102]

Furthermore, Iran's defense ministry would have had no reason to ask researchers to explore for a new method for uranium conversion—quite apart from the fact that uranium conversation was not what military specialists would have been working on in any case. The Atomic Energy Organization of Iran had already begun construction in the late 1990s on the system for uranium conversion it acquired from China, after having tested it for years to make sure it was the right choice for Iran.

There were other indications that the documents were fabrications as well. A subproject under so-called "Project 5" on ore processing mentioned in one of the documents was designated as "Project 5.15". But Iran provided detailed documentation, none of which was contested by the IAEA, showing clearly that the project had actually been approved in August 1999—two years before the start of the alleged secret nuclear weapons program—and

101. Michael Elleman, *Iran's Ballistic Missile Capabilities, A Net Assessment* (London: International Institute for Strategic Studies, 2010), 23-25; Gareth Porter interview with Michael Elleman, November 5, 2010.
102. Prepared statement of Robert D. Walpole, National Intelligence Officer for Strategic and Nuclear Programs, National Intelligence Council, Hearing on September 21, 2000, before the International Security, Proliferation and Federal Services Subcommittee, Senate Committee on Governmental Affairs, 106th Cong., 2nd sess. https://www.govinfo.gov/content/pkg/CHRG-106shrg68305/html/CHRG-106shrg68305.htm; "Excerpts from Internal IAEA Document on Alleged Iranian Nuclear Weaponization," ISIS Repots, Institute for Science an International Security, October 2, 2009, 3; IAEA quarterly report on Iran GOV/2008/15, May 26, 2008, annex, 2.

that it was not run by the IRGC or the Defense Ministry but by the civilian Atomic Energy Organization of Iran itself.[103]

The whole cover story about the documents as coming from a participant/ spy was exploded when the former German Foreign Office's coordinator for North American affairs, Karsten Voigt, revealed how they had actually made their way into the hands of Western intelligence. After his retirement in 2010, Voigt recalled in an interview that senior officials of German intelligence agency, the Bundesnachrichtendienst (BND) had told him in 2004 that those "laptop documents" had been turned over to the BND earlier that year by a member of the Mujahedin-E Khalq, the Iranian terrorist organization.[104]

The senior BND officials further explained to Voigt that they did not trust the source and therefore the reliability of the documents themselves, but they were worried that the George W. Bush administration was basing its policy on them. They were concerned by a statement by Secretary of State Colin Powell that the United States had evidence of Iran seeking to mate a nuclear weapon with its Shahab-3 ballistic missile. Voigt passed on their warning to the Bush administration via an interview with the *Wall Street Journal* a few days later. He was quoted in a *Journal* article as stating flatly that the laptop document had been provided by "an Iranian dissident group" and that the United States and Europe "shouldn't let their Iran policies be influenced by single-source headlines."[105]

There is also good reason to believe that German intelligence agency had warned the CIA not to rely on those documents as evidence. After Powell's remarks, the *Los Angeles Times* reported that some administration officials "were surprised he went public on something that was weak and, *because it was weak, was not supposed to be used* [emphasis added]."[106] After the infamous "Curveball"—an Iraqi who had fled to Germany and told stories of Saddam having "mobile bioweapons labs", the top German intelligence official, August Hanning, had sent a personal message to George Tenet in December 2002 warning him against relying on it as intelligence.[107] Hanning was still

103. IAEA Report, GOV/2008/4, February 22, 2008, 5. https://www.iaea.org/sites/default/files/gov2008-4.pdf.

104. Gareth Porter interview with Karsten Voigt, March 13, 2013.

105. Interview with Voigt; "Bush Pushes His Top Priorities at APEC Meeting," *Wall Street Journal*, November 22, 2004. https://www.wsj.com/articles/SB110095892760179939.

106. Soni Efron, Tyler Marshall and Bob Drogin, "Powell's Talk of Arms Has Fallout," *Los Angeles Times*, November 19, 2004. https://www.latimes.com/archives/la-xpm-2004-nov-19-fg-irannuke19-story.html.

107. "The Spies Who Fooled the World," *BBC Panorama*, March 23, 2013.

the head of BND in late 2004, and the *Los Angeles Times*'s sources' characterization of the documents to which Powell had referred suggests that senior intelligence people were aware of their problematic provenance.

The MEK were well known to have worked for Israel's Mossad intelligence agency by making public information about the Iranian nuclear program that Mossad did not want attributed to itself. And two Israeli authors reported in a book published in 2012 that Mossad had "procured" the collection of laptop documents and shared it with Western intelligence agencies.[108] They failed to mention the fact that Mossad had used the MEK to convey information to Western governments that Israel did not want to be attributed to itself, and that Mossad had created an office in the summer of 2003—just when the laptop documents were being put together—devoted to briefing governments and the media on alleged efforts by Iran to build nuclear weapons, which sometimes passed on documents it claimed had come from Israeli spies.[109]

But the CIA allowed the documents to be used as evidence in making the next National Intelligence Estimate (NIE), despite the fact that analysts had not ruled out fabrication.[110] The NIE issued on the Iran nuclear program in 2005, which was dominated by the technical experts on nuclear weapon at the CIA's Weapons Intelligence, Nonproliferation and Arms Control Center (WINPAC)—the same specialist who had accepted the "Curveball" testimony on alleged mobile weapons laboratories and the aluminum tubes argument against the judgment of most other intelligence analysts. The 2005 had concluded that Iran had an active nuclear weapons program, based in large part on "laptop documents", which WINPAC presumed to be authentic. Thomas Fingar, who was then Chairman of the National Intelligence Council and presided over all such assessments, recalled in an interview that the laptop documents had "cleared up" what had previously been "ambiguity about the purposes of the nuclear program."[111]

The 2007 NIE on Iran's nuclear program is well known for having concluded that Iran had discontinued its nuclear weapons program in 2003.[112]

---

108. Dan Raviv and Yossi Melman, *Spies Against Armageddon: Inside Israel's Secret Wars* (Sea Cliff, N.Y.: Levant Books, 2012), 9.

109. Douglas Frantz and Catherine Colllins, *The Nuclear Jihadist* (New York and Boston: Twelve, 2007), 296-97.

110. Dafna Linzer, "Strong Leads and Dead Ends in Nuclear Case Against Iran," *Washington Post*, February 8, 2006. https://www.kas.de/c/document_library/get_file?uuid=e1f5e496-43bc-2890-6d6a-38e7e734c7cf&groupId=252038.

111. Gareth Porter interview with Thomas Fingar, Oxford, UK, February 7, 2013.

112. See Appendices Document No. 1, National Intelligence Estimate, "Iran: Nuclear Intentions and Capabilities," November 2007.

In mid-2007, however, the analysts had approved a draft that changed none of the key judgments of the 2005 NIE, according to Fingar. It was only after the CIA had obtained intercepted messages and other data in which military research figures complained about work that analysts presumed to be related to nuclear weapons that had been terminated that the original draft was revised to conclude that the presumed nuclear weapons work had been stopped, as Fingar recounted. The final text of the NIE said it could not determine whether Iran "currently intends to develop nuclear weapons", although it suggested that it was "less determined" than was previously judged.

The CIA's 2007 National Intelligence Estimate's conclusion that Iran had terminated a covert nuclear weapons program in 2003 represented more of a continuity with the agency's questionable past approach to the Iran nuclear issue than a break with it. It was explicitly based on the erroneous assumption that the documents foisted on the West by Israel were authentic. Thus, the policies adopted by both the Obama administration and the Trump administration toward Iran have reflected the intelligence community's continued reliance on a set of fabricated documents as the basis for claiming that Iran is pursuing nuclear weapons. And that fateful CIA error has now led the Trump administration to embark on a foolish and reckless confrontation with Iran.

4. From Nuclear Deal to "Maximum Pressure"

Why Obama's Nuclear Deal Didn't Survive

THE NUCLEAR DEAL STRUCK BY THE Obama administration with Iran in 2015 appeared to represent a break with the decades-long official U.S. hostility toward Iran. But in fact, it also represented continuity in the official attitude toward the Islamic Republic. The story of how it came about and why the Trump administration renounced it goes to the heart of the fundamental political dynamics that continue to propel the United States toward a fateful military confrontation with Iran.

The dominant political narrative surrounding the Joint Comprehensive Plan of Action (JCPOA) is that the agreement reflected the Obama administration's successful use of "coercive diplomacy" in getting international support for sanctions against Iran's banking and oil sectors. That narrative explains the outcome as the result of economic pressure on the Iranian government that lead to the Iranian reform candidate Hasan Rouhani winning the 2013 Presidential race.

There is another side of the story, however, that more accurately explains the nuclear agreement. It is the story of how Iran deployed its own "enrichment diplomacy"—the threat of going further up the scale of enrichment—to resist U.S. pressure and to build effective diplomatic pressure on the Obama administration to allow Iran to continue its enrichment program—albeit at a much lower level—under the agreement.

The Iranian negotiating approach was based on the idea that a program of uranium enrichment would represent not only a symbol of Iran's independence and scientific advancement but a source of diplomatic leverage on the United States without which Iran would be unable to get the United

States to end the economic sanctions and other elements of aggressively hostile U.S. policy toward Iran. Long before Iran began actually enriching uranium, Iran's national security officials were thinking of enrichment as a diplomatic asset. Iranian political scientist Jalil Rosendel, who worked on a research project on nuclear power and national security for the Iranian Foreign Ministry's think tank in 1997-98 and later taught at East Carolina State University, recalled that influential figures he interviewed believed a uranium enrichment program would provide negotiating leverage with the Americans to win the removal of the U.S. sanctions that had just been imposed.[113]

In March 2005—the year before a single centrifuge had begun to enrich uranium—Iran sought to parlay its potential future stockpile of enriched uranium into a deal for U.S. security guarantees and an end to economic sanctions. They had hoped that the interest of the three main European allies of the United States—the UK, France, and Germany—would help bring such a deal to fruition. The Bush administration vetoed the idea of any deal that would allow Iranian enrichment, and the EU three were forced by U.S. pressure to refuse even to discuss it further.[114]

Barack Obama had campaigned on a platform that included a pledge to negotiate with Iran, but once in the White House, he embraced the traditional U.S. approach by using military threats and economic pressure to try to force Iran to give up its nuclear program. Obama's Secretary of State, Hillary Clinton, told Congress in April 2009 that the administration viewed "the diplomatic path" as a way to "gain credibility and influence with a number of nations who would have to participate in order make the sanctions regime as tight and crippling as we want it to be."[115]

Obama's initial coercive effort was the first ever cyberattack resulting in damage to infrastructure in human history. Shortly after taking office, he approved the planning for a cyberattack on Iran's enrichment plant at Natanz called Olympic Games, and then approved the actual attack on the facility carried out in June 2009.[116] Meanwhile, the Obama administration

---

113. Gareth Porter interview with Jalil Roshandel, May 13, 2013.
114. Porter, *Manufactured Crisis*, 153-157.
115. New Beginnings: Foreign Policy Priorities in the Obama Administration: Hearings on April 22, 2009, before the House Committee on Foreign Affairs, 111th Cong. 2nd sess., testimony of Secretary of State Hillary Rodham Clinton (Washington, D.C.: Government Printing Office, 2009), 19, 22.
116. David Sanger, "Obama's Order Sped Up Wave of Cyberattacks against Iran," *New York Times*, June 1, 2012; James Bamford, "The Secret War," *Wired*, June 12, 2012.

was exploiting the threats of an Israeli attack on Iranian nuclear facilities that Benjamin Netanyahu continued to make between 2009 and 2012, mainly through leaks to the press. Those threats were not really credible, because of the fact, known to administration insiders, that the Israeli air force could not carry out a successful attack on those facilities without U.S. approval and involvement. But Obama and his advisers hoped such fears would cause UN Security members such as France and China to support much tougher financial sanctions on Iran that would succeed in forcing Iran to give up its enrichment program.[117]

Obama's main form of pressure on Iran to give up its nuclear program was a new form of sanctions against any foreign firms doing business with Iran. The new sanctions took advantage of language that the Obama administration insisted on inserting into the United Nations Security Council Resolution 1929, adopted in June 2010, which the Treasury Department then used to broaden the U.S. use of extraordinary sanctions against foreign banks and other firms by threatening them with being linked indirectly to alleged Iran nuclear and missile activities.

Obama got the European allies to adopt similar sanctions on oil and banking transactions in 2012.[118]

The effect was to cut deeply into Iran's foreign currency earnings and throw its economy into reverse gear. But Iran had its own diplomatic strategy that revolved around exploiting its ability to enrich uranium to 20 percent. Iran began enrichment to 20 percent in early 2010, after the Obama administration had ignored its threat to do so if the United States refused to allow Iran to purchase the amount of that 20 percent enriched uranium necessary for fuel rods for Iran's Tehran research reactor for making medical isotopes. But enrichment to 20 percent is also a big step toward weapons grade enrichment (90 percent), and it was bound to create political pressure on the Obama administration to do something to reverse it.

After talks between Iran and the coalition called the P5+1 began in 2012, Iran made it clear through its decisions on enrichment and centrifuge deployment that it had the *capability* to achieve what U.S. experts considered

---

117. For a detailed account of Netanyahu's elaborate ploys to convey the impression he was prepared to attack Iran, the evidence that it was never genuine and the exploitation of that threat by the Obama administration to put pressure on Iran, see Porter, *Manufactured Crisis*, 269-292.

118. For a description of the manipulative and deceptive methods used by the Treasury Department's Stuart Levey to intimidate foreign banks in particular, see Chapter 6, p. 79. The language inserted in UN Security Council Resolution 1929 for that purpose is in Document No. 3 in the Appendices of this book.

a "break-out" to a nuclear weapon—the amount of 20 percent uranium necessary for enrichment to weapons-grade level for a single nuclear weapon. But at the same time, it also made it clear that its *intent* was to give the Obama administration a strong incentive to negotiate on Iran's demands for its basic nuclear rights and the removal of sanctions. Iran then proceeded to curb the growth of its stockpile of 20-percent enriched uranium by converting a large part of it to powder for fuel plates to be used by the Tehran research reactor. Between late 2011 and February 2013, Iran had enriched 280 kg to 20 percent, which would have put it well over the level regarded by some as a "breakout" capability, but it had also converted 113 kg—40 percent of that total—to powder for fuel plates, leaving only 167 kg in the form of 20 percent enriched uranium in the stockpile.[119]

Meanwhile, the number of centrifuges available for enrichment to 20 percent at the Fordow enrichment facility had roughly doubled between May and August 2012, but none of the newly installed centrifuges were enriching uranium; they were not even connected with pipes. In fact, only one third of the centrifuges that were connected were enriching.[120]

The Obama administration clearly understood the Iranian message. "They are creating tremendous capacity, but they are not using it," a senior U.S. official told the *New York Times*, noting that the pattern of centrifuge deployment gave the Iranians "leverage"—obviously referring to nuclear talks to come.[121] The Iranian message was further reinforced in September 2012 when Iran offered to halt its enrichment to 20 percent, in return for easing sanctions against Iran.[122] In fact, it was only after Iran had sent those signals that Iran agreed to negotiations with the Obama administration to begin after the elections. Furthermore, senior Obama administration officials

---

119. International Atomic Energy Agency, "Implementation of the NPT Safeguards Agreement and relevant provisions of Security Council resolutions in the Islamic Republic of Iran," GOV/2013/6, February 21, 2013, 3. https://www.iaea.org/sites/default/files/gov2013-6.pdf

120. David Albright, Christina Walrond, Andrea Stricker, and Robert Avagyan, "ISIS Analysis of IAEA Iran Safeguards Report," ISIS, August 30, 2012, p. 4. http://isis-online.org/uploads/isis-reports/documents/ISIS_Analysis_IAEA_Report_30Aug2012.pdf

121. David J. Sanger and William J. Broad, "Inspectors Confirm New Work by Iran at Secure Nuclear Site," *New York Times*, August 30, 2012. https://www.nytimes.com/2012/08/31/world/middleeast/nuclear-inspectors-confirm-iranian-progress.html.

122. Gareth Porter, "Iranian Diplomat Says Iran Offered Deal to Halt 20-Percent Enrichment," *Inter Press Service*, September 24, 2012. http://www.ipsnews.net/2012/09/iranian-diplomat-says-iran-offered-deal-to-halt-20-percent-enrichment/.

began discussing internally the possibility of agreement allowing a very limited enrichment program as part of a settlement with Iran after the Iranian signaling had been carried out.[123]

The Obama administration's decision to give up the long-established U.S. demand that Iran must abandon even the most peaceful and thoroughly monitored nuclear program paved the way for the 2015 nuclear deal agreement, the Joint Comprehensive Program of Action (JCPOA). The deal required that for 15 years Iran would have to limit enrichment to 3.67 percent, reduce its stockpile of low enriched uranium to 300kg, permanently end 20 percent enrichment and make major changes in its Arak reactor—all under the most elaborate system of monitoring and control to which any country had ever submitted. It also required that the United States cease the of application of all economic sanctions against the oil and banking sectors of Iran as well as an end to all UN Security Council resolutions that had targeted the Iranian nuclear program and their attendant economic sanctions.[124]

The JCPOA had the support of the U.S. national security elite and of the Democratic Party, and most new media were not overtly hostile to it. But the Iran deal had two fatal political vulnerabilities that would prove to be its undoing: The first was that the Israeli government of Prime Minister Benjamin Netanyahu was determined to derail the agreement, and it had the overweening political power over the U.S. Congress in regard to Iran to do just that. The American Israel Public Affairs Committee (AIPAC), the main Israel lobby in Washington, had given top priority for years in its Congressional work to preventing any agreement with Iran, and it was able to mobilize majorities in both houses of Congress for the demand that Congress be able to accept or reject the agreement. Meanwhile, the Foundation for the Defense of Democracies, a pro-Israel think-tank focused primarily on influencing U.S. policy toward Iran, was leading the propaganda assault on the agreement.[125] The rejection of the JCPOA in the House of Representatives on September 11, 2015 by a vote of 269 to 162 showed dramatically how

---

123. Helene Cooper and Mark Landler, "U.S. Officials Say Iran Has Agreed to Nuclear Talks," *New York Times*, October 20, 2012. https://www.nytimes.com/2012/10/21/world/iran-said-ready-to-talk-to-us-about-nuclear-program.html.

124. The Joint Comprehensive Plan of Action is arguably the most complex international agreement in the history of diplomacy. For a summary of the commitments undertaken by Iran and by the other signatories under the agreement, see "The Joint Comprehensive Plan of Action (JCPOA) at a Glance," Arms Control Association, May 2018. https://www.armscontrol.org/factsheets/JCPOA-at-a-glance.

125. Eli Clifton and Ali Gharib, "How the Anti-Iran Lobby Machine Dominate Capitol Hill," *The Nation*, July 15, 2014. https://www.thenation.com/article/how-anti-iran-lobby-machine-dominates-capitol-hill/.

completely U.S policy was subject to a special interest group that disposed the money and organization necessary to line up Congress behind its position.

The Obama administration's vulnerability to the Israeli-inspired assault on the JCPOA was magnified, moreover, by its inability to contest the main argument that would be used to discredit the agreement—that the JCPOA would not prevent Iran from getting a nuclear weapon but would only delay it for some years. The Obama administration had based its entire Iran policy on the assumption that Iran did indeed want nuclear weapons and had to be restrained by the pressure of economic sanctions to give it up, at least temporarily. The only supposed evidence for that accusation—the so-called "laptop documents"—had been forged rather crudely. But no one in the Obama administration had ever entertained the slightest doubt about the entire Iran nuclear narrative that had been woven during the George W. Bush administration. The Obama administration was not part of the solution to the Iran nuclear crisis but part of the problem

Bringing Iran to its Knees

DONALD TRUMP'S ENTRY INTO THE OVAL Office in 2017, combined with Israeli and pro-Israeli Americans' influence on Trump's policy, led to the adoption of the most aggressive U.S. government posture toward Iran in the entire history of the conflict. Trump's policy was inevitably shaped by his personal and financial ties with extremist pro-Israel figures. Trump's son-in-law Jared Kushner's father was a longtime supporter and personal friend of Netanyahu's as well as an ardent supporter of Israeli settlements on the occupied West Bank.[126] But even more important, the biggest single contribution to his campaign—$100 million—had come from Sheldon Adelson, the extremist Zionist opponent of the deal who held dual U.S. and Israeli citizenship and had also bankrolled Netanyahu's past presidential campaigns as well.[127]

Netanyahu exploited the opportunity to the hilt. In a speech before the

---

126. Jodi Kantor, "For Kushner, Israel Policy May Be Shaped by the Personal," *New York Times*, February 11, 2017. https://www.nytimes.com/2017/02/11/us/politics/jared-kushner-israel.html.
127. "Adelson set to give over $100 million to Israel-supporting Trump," *Times of Israel*, May 14, 2016. https://www.timesofisrael.com/adelson-set-to-give-over-100-million-to-israel-supporting-trump/.

UN General Assembly in September 2017, he declared, "Israel's policy toward the nuclear deal is very simple: Change it or cancel it. Fix it or nix it." Netanyahu continued, "Nixing the deal means restoring massive pressure on Iran, including crippling sanctions, until Iran fully dismantles its nuclear weapons capability." As for "fixing" it, he demanded an end to the "sunset clause"—meaning that Iran could never resume enrichment for a nuclear power program—as well as an end to the development of Iran's ballistic missile program and the "roll back" of Iran's "growing aggression in the region."[128]

As Trump was preparing for his first major policy statement on the Iran deal, he wasn't listening to Secretary of Defense James Mattis or Secretary of State Rex Tillerson, who were against tearing it up. He was listening instead to John Bolton, the longtime advocate of aggressive war on Iran and also client of Adelson. It was Bolton who called Trump from Las Vegas after meeting with Adelson to suggest that Trump include in his remarks a flat statement that he could withdraw from the pact at any time.[129]

In his Iran policy statement in October 2017, Trump followed the Netanyahu script closely. He vowed to "work with our allies to counter the regime's destabilizing activity and support for terrorist proxies in the region." Then he announced plans to work with Congressional leaders on legislation that would require making the JCPOA's nuclear restrictions on Iran permanent and go after Iran's missile program. And he warned that if either Congress or the European allies refused to agree to the changes, he could withdraw the United States from the agreement "at any time"—just as Bolton had suggested. And he went beyond any of his predecessors in demonizing Iran, which he said was "under the control of a fanatical regime" that had "spread death, destruction and chaos all around the globe."[130]

Despite Trump's October 2017 statement, Netanyahu was afraid that Trump might be steered by the three major European allies, national security adviser H. R. McMaster and Secretary of State Rex Tillerson to stay in the JCPOA. Trump had told Netanyahu before the 2016 election that he would cancel the nuclear agreement, but Netanyahu acknowledged to

128. PM Netanyahu the United Nations General Assembly," September 1, 2017. https://mfa.gov.il/MFA/PressRoom/2017/Pages/PM-Netanyahu-addresses-the-United-Nations-General-Assembly-19-September-2017.aspx.

129. Eliana Johnson, "Nikki Haley was Trump's Iran Whisperer," *Politico*, October 13, 2017. https://www.politico.com/story/2017/10/13/nikki-haley-trump-iran-whisperer-243772

130. "Remarks by President Trump on Iran Strategy," October 13, 2017. See Document No. 4 in the Appendices to this book.

the *New York Times* in August 2019 that he had not counted on Trump to follow through and had sought to "bolster the decision".[131] His "bolstering" operation turned out to be an elaborate plan to reveal an alleged Iranian secret "nuclear archive" in that Netanyahu claimed in 2018 Mossad had miraculously discovered and stolen from in a warehouse right in the heart of Tehran.

Netanyahu's theatrical presentation showed what he said were documents proving that Iran had an maintained an ongoing active nuclear weapons program—all based on the claim that Mossad had broken into a highly secret Tehran warehouse and stolen more than 100,000 documents weighing half a ton from what he called Iran's "nuclear archive".[132] The fundamental premise of Netanyahu's show was that Iran had placed every document having to do with its alleged nuclear weapons program in an unguarded Tehran warehouse that could easily be broken into, and that Israel's Mossad had known precisely where to find it. Those claims were implausible on their face. There was no reason whatsoever for the Defense Ministry to move any documents that had been under its control from its own offices—much less documents supposedly showing an unacknowledged program to acquire nuclear weapons.

In his slideshow, moreover, Netanyahu displayed the same crude schematic drawing of an Iranian Shahab-3 missile with a circle in the reentry vehicle representing a nuclear weapon that had turned up in the cache of documents used by the Bush administration to convince the media and the international community that Iran had a nuclear weapons program from 2000 to 2003.[133] That was one of the crucial documents that gave away the fabricated character of the entire collection, because Iran's defense ministry had given up on the Shahab-3 depicted in that drawing at least two years before the start of the alleged top secret nuclear weapons program was said to have started. And the new missile that went into development to replace the Shahab-3 design had a reentry vehicle that had a "baby bottle" shape completely different from the "dunce cap" shape of the original.[134]

---

131. Ronen Bergman and Mark Mazzetti, "The Secret History of the Push to Strike Iran," *New York Times Magazine*, September 4, 2019. https://www.nytimes.com/2019/09/04/magazine/iran-strike-israel-america.html.

132. For the complete video of Netanyahu's show see "Israeli PM Netanyahu Reveals Documents Proving Iranian Nuclear Program; Deal Is Based On 'Deception'," *Real Clear Politics*, April 30, 2018. https://www.realclearpolitics.com/video/2018/04/30/israeli_pm_netanyahu_reveals_proof_of_secret_iranian_nuclear_program.html.

133. The schematic drawing of the missile, appears in the Netanyahu video at 6:57.

134. See chapter 3, pp. 43-44.

On May 8, 2018, Trump announced that he was withdrawing the United States from the JCPOA, because Iran and the other members of the P5+1 had refused to renegotiate the pact to satisfy Trump's demands. Trump also announced that he was ready to negotiate on a bilateral basis with Iran on a new deal. He acknowledged that the Iranians had rejected any such negotiations, but suggested they would have to come around anyway.[135]

Behind that decision was a seismic shift in the Trump administration's national security team engineered by pro-Israel lobbyists in Washington to get the personnel they wanted to ensure a U.S. policy of confrontation with Iran. In the short space of a few days in March 2018, both H. R. McMaster and Rex Tillerson were fired, opening the way for John Bolton and Mike Pompeo to carry out a much more aggressive policy toward Iran. The Tillerson decision was the result of lobbying by pro-Israel and pro-Saudi forces who attacked Tillerson for his opposition to a UAE-led embargo against Qatar that was also supported by Israel. But it was also a strategic move to eliminate a key obstacle to taking the United States out of the JCPOA. When the firing of Tillerson was announced, Mark Dubowitz, the CEO of the Foundation for the Defense of Democracies, who had played a key role in defeating the nuclear deal with Iran, triumphantly tweeted the news and theatrically copied the tweet to Iran's Supreme Leader Khamenei and President Rouhani. He was publicly hinting at the full-scale Trump administration attack on the Iranian economy that the replacement of Tillerson by Mike Pompeo was about to bring about.[136]

Both Bolton and Pompeo were eager to align U.S. Iran policy with Israel's interests in weakening even overthrowing the Islamic regime and engineering a military conflict between the United States and Iran. Bolton had long called for U.S. bombing of Iran, and openly served as a cheerleader for regime change by the Mujahideen-E Khalq (MEK) at an MEK rally in Paris in July 2017. He had ended his speech by declaring dramatically, "Before 2019, we here will celebrate in Tehran."[137]

Pompeo was an unusually ambitious figure with both political and religious motives for backing Israel's new provocative strategy toward Iran. He had recognized by 2016 that the combination of financial backing by

---

135. "Remarks by President Trump on the Joint Comprehensive Plan of Action," May 8, 2018. https://www.whitehouse.gov/briefings-statements/remarks-president-trump-joint-comprehensive-plan-action/.
136. Mark Perry, "The Political Forces Behind Rex Tillerson's Firing," *The American Conservative*, March 25, 2018. https://www.theamericanconservative.com/articles/the-political-forces-behind-rex-tillersons-firing/.
137. https://twitter.com/BahmanKalbasi/status/976968096908021760

Zionist billionaires like Adelson and tens of millions of Christian Zionist voters in the United States were his ticket to political power. He had then seized on the Iran nuclear deal as the issue that would propel his political career, aligning himself initially with Sen. Marco Rubio, who already had the backing for his primary campaign for the Republican nomination.[138] And Pompeo had joined the Evangelical Presbyterian Church, which believes in "the Rapture"—the "End Time" event accompanying the second coming of Christ that has made millions of American Christian fervent supporters of Zionism and Israel and belligerent foes of Iran.[139]

Trump had only the foggiest idea what it would mean to negotiate a new deal with Iran, and that gave Pompeo and Bolton the opportunity to use the pretense of a new deal to push their real agenda: to create circumstances favoring regime change and/or military confrontation with Iran. On May 21, Pompeo vowed in a speech at the Heritage Foundation that once the sanctions the administration was already planning took hold, Iran "will be battling to keep its economy alive". Then he presented a list of twelve demands on Iran that would have to be fulfilled to end those sanctions that constituted in effect a demand for Iran's surrender—not only in regard to its security, but in regard to its very exercise of sovereignty.[140]

The primary demands were that Iran end its ballistic missile program, end its support for Hezbollah, Hamas, Palestinian Islamic Jihad and the Houthis ,and withdraw all Iranian-controlled forces from Syria. Those demands implied that the Trump administration believed that it would soon be in a position to dictate to Iran as a defeated state, as it had been able to do to Iraq after its defeat in the first Gulf War. That was the meaning of UN Security Council Resolution 687 requiring all Iraqi ballistic missiles with a range over 150 kilometers to be destroyed or removed under international supervision. The assumption underlying Pompeo's 12 points was thus that

138. Susan B. Glasser, "Mike Pompeo, the Secretary of Trump," *The New Yorker*, August 19, 2019. https://www.newyorker.com/magazine/2019/08/26/mike-pompeo-the-secretary-of-trump; number of Christian Zionist voters in Mimi Kirk, "Countering Christian Zionism in the Age of Trump," Lobelog, August 19, 2019. https://lobelog.com/countering-christian-zionism-in-the-age-of-trump/.
139. Edward Wong, "The Rapture and the Real World: Mike Pompeo Blends Beliefs and Policy," *New York Times*, March 30, 2019. https://www.nytimes.com/2019/03/30/us/politics/pompeo-christian-policy.html. Significantly Pompeo's own church does not take a position on the issue of whether the "End Time" of the second coming of Christ requires a war in "Armageddon" (i.e., Israel) as the Christian Zionist movement believes.
140. Secretary of State Michael R. Pompeo, "After the Deal: A New Iran Strategy," May 21, 2018. https://www.state.gov/after-the-deal-a-new-iran-strategy/.

the new sanctions that the administration was working on would similarly bring Iran to its knees by preventing it from being able to export enough to maintain a viable economy.

Pompeo even brazenly warned the Iranian people that they would have to either take matters into their own hands to get a government that would give in to U.S. demands or suffer the consequences of punitive U.S. sanctions. "[A]t the end of the day," he said, "the Iranian people will decide the timeline…. If they make the decision quickly, that would be wonderful. If they choose not to do so, we will stay hard at this until we achieve the outcomes that I set today."

Bolton denied that the administration was pursuing "regime change" in Iran.[141] That may well have been literally true, in the sense that there was no document that stated that explicit goal, and Trump would not have approved such a policy. But Trump's foreign policymaking under Bolton was notorious for avoidance of formal policy papers, and in treating Iran as though it could be reduced to the status of Iraq after the first Gulf War, the Bolton-Pompeo duo were essentially pursuing just such an aim.

Weakening Regional Deterrence

IN A SPEECH LAYING OUT THE Trump administration's demands on Iran, Pompeo portrayed Iran as destabilizing the entire region by "fueling proxy wars across the Middle East".[142] That had become standard language in both official comment and media coverage on Iranian policy even before Trump entered the White House. But an examination of the historical and current realities surrounding Iran's arming of its allies in Lebanon, Syria, Iraq and Yemen reveals that the Iranian role was stabilizing rather than destabilizing and that it has been aimed at deterring the United States and Israel from attacking Iran itself.

"Hizbullah is now armed to the teeth by Iran and has set its sights on Israel," Pompeo declared. In fact, however, no serious analyst believes that the arming of Hezbollah has ever been intended to allow Hezbollah to plan

---

141. Rebecca Morin, "Bolton says U.S. not seeking Iranian regime change," *Politico*, August 6, 2018. https://www.politico.com/story/2018/08/06/john-bolton-iran-sanctions-regime-change-764605.

142. Speech by Secretary of State Mike Pompeo at AEI, May 21, 2018. See Document No. 7 in Appendices to this book.

to initiate a war with Israel. On the contrary, the arming of Hezbollah has been aimed at the maintenance of long-lasting mutual deterrence between Israel and Hezbollah. After all, for many years, the Israeli Defense Forces (IDF) assessment has been clear that Hezbollah leader Nasrallah is firmly committed to maintaining a state of mutual deterrence.[143]

Pompeo asserted that Iran's intervention in Syria "perpetuates" the conflict, thus making Syria "71,000 square miles of kill zone". But that tricky formulation obscured the fundamental historical reality of the Syrian War: that it was the U.S.'s regional allies—Turkey, Qatar and Saudi Arabia—whose intervention, beginning in 2012 with the Obama's administration' approval and support, that turned the Syrian conflict into a major internationalized conventional war by injecting tens of thousands of tons of conventional weapons into Syria and allowed al Qaeda's Syrian franchise to achieve a dominant role in the war.[144] Only after that intervention had already transformed the war into a jihadist-dominated campaign did Iran and Hezbollah intervene militarily, helping to preserve a Syrian state apparatus that was brutal and repressive but was regarded by the U.S. military and CIA as necessary to prevent complete chaos and jihadist takeover of the entire country.[145]

Pompeo's accusation that Iran "sponsored Shi'a groups and terrorists to infiltrate and undermine Iraqi security forces and jeopardize Iraqi sovereignty" is a whopper of epic proportions. He is obviously referring to Iraqi militia organizations aligned with Iranian views on the region, which belong to a broad national coalition called the "Popular Mobilization Forces" (PMU). That coalition, with training and advice by Iranians led by Gen. Qasem Soleimani, head of the IRGC Quds Force, played a crucial role in the fight against the Islamic State from 2014 until its ultimate defeat in 2018. Furthermore, it was the failure of the Iraqi Army that created the need for the PMU to intervene. And that Iran-supported PMU role saved Iraq from a

---

143. Carmit Valensi and Yoram Schweitzer, "Hezbollah's Concept of Deterrence according Nasrallah: From the Second Lebanon War to the Present," in *The Quiet Decade: the Aftermath of the Second Lebanon War, 2006-2016*, Udi Dekel, Gabi Siboni, and Omer Einav, eds. (Tel Aviv: Institute for National Security Studies, 2017), 115-127; Udi Dekel and Assaf Orion, "The Next War against ': Strategic and Operational Considerations," The Quiet Decade, 140.
144. Gareth Porter, "How America Armed Terrorists in Syria," *The American Conservative*, June 22, 2017. https://www.theamericanconservative.com/articles/how-america-armed-terrorists-in-syria/
145. Seymour Hersh, "Military to Military," *London Review of Books*, January 7, 2016. https://www.lrb.co.uk/v38/n01/seymour-m-hersh/military-to-military.

major threat to its territorial integrity.[146] So Pompeo's characterization of the Iranian role in Iraq can only be characterized as grotesquely false, regardless of how unpopular Iran's considerable influence in Iraq has become.

As for Yemen, Pompeo claimed that the Houthi militia who have gotten Iranian arms since the beginning of the indiscriminate Saudi-led bombing campaign "fuels a conflict that continues to starve the Yemeni people and hold them under the threat of terror." But as Pompeo must certainly be aware, it is more than six years of Saudi coalition bombing that "continues to starve" Yemenis and keeps them "under the threat of terror".

A closer analysis of Iran's alliances with Hezbollah, the Assad government, the Houthis and the pro-Iran militias in Iraq, which Pompeo and the Israelis have sought to portray as Iranian "destabilization" across the region, reveals a very different phenomenon: an Iranian effort over nearly two decades to establish a crude and unorthodox form of deterrence of the United States and Israel. That form of deterrence was necessary to make up for Iran's own serious weakness in both aircraft and missiles. The only means it had to achieve effective deterrence was to provide arms to non-state allies who could threaten to use them against Israel or U.S. military targets in the region if Iran were attacked.

The Iranian strategy of deterrence began in response to explicit Israeli threats to attack its nuclear and missile programs in the mid- to late 1990s, when Iran was still desperately trying to develop a reliable ballistic missile deterrent. In the late 1990s, Iran's Defense Ministry came to the realization that the Shahab-3 ballistic missile it had hoped would provide its deterrence fell well short of the need, and that an improved version of the missile would lack the numbers, accuracy and secure firing positions necessary to reliably deter Israeli or U.S. attack for many years.[147]

As a result, Iran was forced to rely on a strategy of giving regional allies the capability to hit Israeli and U.S. targets. At first Tehran had only Hezbollah and Syria. It soon began sending rockets and missiles to Hezbollah by air and by sea to its ally Syria, from where they were trucked the short distance to Lebanon. Those rockets gave both Hezbollah and Syria the capability to retaliate against at least part of Israel if either the United States or Israel

---

146. Alireza Nader, *Iran's Role in Iraq: Room for U.S.-Iran Cooperation?* Rand Corporation, 2005.https://www.rand.org/content/dam/rand/pubs/perspectives/PE100/PE151/RAND_PE151.pdf.

147. Frederick Wehrey et al, *Dangerous but Not Omnipotent: Exploring the Reach and Limitations of Iranian Power in the Middle East* (Santa Monica: RAND Corporation, 2009), 59. https://www.rand.org/content/dam/rand/pubs/monographs/2009/RAND_MG781.pdf; Porter, *Manufactured Crisis*, 42-45.

attacked Iran.[148] By the time Israel launched its second invasion of Lebanon in 2006, Israeli intelligence estimated that Hezbollah had an arsenal of 12,000-18,000 missiles, some of which were able to reach more than 140 km into Israel and thus to threaten Haifa, Israel's third largest city.[149]

After the Israeli invasion of Lebanon had been defeated, however, Iran went much further in building a Hezbollah deterrent. It helped Syria establish the domestic production facilities and equipment for what the Syrians called M-600 missiles, much of which were to be passed on to Hezbollah.[150] By 2010, after Iran further built up and modernized the Hezbollah deterrent, Israeli military intelligence estimated publicly that Iran had transferred hundreds of M-600 missiles with 250 km range and much increased accuracy to Hezbollah through Syria, meaning that they could now reach Tel Aviv.[151]

After Saudi Arabia, Qatar and Turkey launched a campaign with U.S. blessing to overthrow the Assad regime in Syria in 2012, Israel began carrying out regular air attacks on convoys carrying missiles to Lebanon. Despite the Israeli attacks, however, Iran introduced more accurate versions of the M-600 with longer ranges, and by 2017, Israeli intelligence estimated the Hezbollah arsenal at 100,000 missiles and rockets.[152]

Iran also cultivated ties with three Iraqi Shi'a militias that were aligned with its views, all of which joined the "Popular Mobilization Forces" semi-official coalition of mostly Shi'a organizations formed in 2014 to fight the Islamic State. In response to the announcement by the Trump administration that sanctions would be fully reimposed in 2018, Iran reportedly sent short-range missiles to its Iraqi allies as part of its broader regional deterrence

148. NTI, "Syria/Missiles". https://www.nti.org/learn/countries/syria/delivery-systems/; "Iran Supplies improved rockets to Syria and Hezbollah, Jane's Missiles and Rockets, September 22, 2004. https://archive.is/20120707043131/http://articles.janes.com/articles/Janes-Missiles-And-Rockets-2004/Iran-supplies-improved-rockets-to-Syria-and-Hizbullah.html.
149. Eyal Zisser, "A Decade of Decision: Lebanon and Syria from the Second Lebanon War to the Syrian Civil War," in Dekel, Sibini and Einav, eds, *The Quiet Decade*, 100.
150. NTI, "Syria/Missiles".
151. Yaakov Katz and Rebecca Anna Stoil, "Hizbullah Received Hundreds of Syrian Missiles," *Jerusalem Post*, May 5, 2010. https://www.jpost.com/Middle-East/Hizbullah-received-hundreds-of-Syrian-missiles.
152. Zisser, "A Decade of Decision," 110.

strategy, which would in theory give them the capability to retaliate against U.S. military bases in Iraq in the event of a U.S. attack on Iran.[153]

After the Saudi-led coalition launched its air war against the Houthis in Yemen in March 2015, Iran added the Houthis to its deterrence network. The IRGC began providing the Houthis with the components for a wide range of advanced missiles and drones, including a drone that has a range of 1,200-1,500 km and could drop an 18-kg bomb on a target, according to a UN panel of experts who examined six of them in 2018. That brings Riyadh and a range of military targets in Saudi Arabia and other Gulf states within its range.[154]

For many years, Iran has remained silent about its efforts to establish such a deterrent based on arming its regional allies. But in late August 2019, former Iranian Deputy Foreign Minister Hossein Sheikholeslam, who is an adviser to Foreign Minister Mohammad Javad Zarif, provided the first explicit public acknowledgement of that Iranian regional deterrent strategy. Citing figures he claimed had been made by Netanyahu and the Americans, Sheikholeslam said that 150,000 Iranian missiles are now "deployed in Lebanon, Syria and Gaza—which Iran has the prerogative to activate," that they could be "launched on Iran's order" and that they "target Israel". He further revealed for the first time that Iran assumes that these missiles would also deter the United States, given its close ties to Israel.[155]

Sheikholeslam declared that these missiles "constitute our greatest deterrence against America and Israel," implicitly acknowledging that Iran's own official deterrent force of medium-range missiles alone is still inadequate to deter its adversaries. He added that Iran wanted the United States and Israel "to know that we have this capability", meaning that his revelation was intended to make its deterrent strategy explicit for the first time.

Whether anyone in the Trump administration understands the distinction between the Iranian effort to deter U.S. or Israeli attack and an aggressive policy aimed at dominating the region and threatening Israel is unclear.

---

153. John Irish and Ahmed Rasheed, "Exclusive: Iran moves missiles to Iraq in warning to enemies," *Reuters*, August 31, 2018. https://www.reuters .com/article/us-iran-iraq-missiles-exclusive/exclusive-iran-moves-missiles-to-iraq-in-warning-to-enemies-idUSKCN1LG0WB.

154. Final Report of UN Panel of Experts on Yemen (S/2019/83), January 29, 2019, 30. https://reliefweb.int/sites/reliefweb.int/files/resources/S_2019_83_E.pdf

155. "Senior Iranian Official Hossein Sheikholeslam: 150,000 Missiles in Lebanon, Syria Gaza Are Meant to Deter Israel and the U.S.," MEMRI TV (Middle East Media Research Institute TV Monitor Project), Clip No. 7448, August 27, 2019. https:// www.memri.org/tv/senior-iranian-official-hossein-sheikholeslam-150000-missile-stockpile-near-israel-deterrence-strategy.

And it is virtually certain that Trump himself has no such understanding. But the Israeli government clearly understands that fact very well, and the Israeli military offensive against Iranian and allied targets in the region in 2018-19 is not aimed at stabilizing deterrence between Iran and Israel. Rather, it is aimed at inflicting as much damage on the Iranian strategy as possible.

5. Pushing for War with Iran

IN DECEMBER 2017, A DELEGATION OF senior Israeli national security officials met secretly with their American counterparts at the White House
for two full days and reached an unprecedented U.S.-Israeli agreement on
a joint U.S.-Israeli "work plan" for countering Iran. A key element in the
agreement, according to an authoritative report by an Israeli journalist whose
sources revealed the exact wording, was a working group for "joint preparation" for "different escalation scenarios in the region, concerning Iran, Syria,
Hezbollah in Lebanon and Hamas in Gaza."[156]

The "escalation scenarios" to which it referred were clearly primarily scenarios having to do with military escalation that the Israelis were already
planning. The Netanyahu government's plan was to take advantage of the
close relationship between Trump and Israeli President Benjamin Netanyahu
to get U.S. support for a major Israeli military escalation against Iran and its
allied forces across the Middle East.

That secret meeting marked a new phase of Israeli efforts not only to
influence but to shape U.S. policy toward Iran. Ironically, during a period in
which U.S. political life was focused overwhelmingly on the alleged threat
of Russian intervention and undue influence on U.S. elections and policy,
Israel was seeking unprecedented leverage over the central issue of war and
peace with Iran. The Israeli strategy was never discussed in corporate media

---

156. Barak Ravid, "Scoop: U.S. and Israel reach joint plan to counter Iran," *Axios*,
December 26, 2017. https://www.axios.com/scoop-us-and-israel-reach-joint-plan-
to-counter-iran-1515110887-51be0529-3ff5-4d8f-89f1-6c89423d4dff.html

coverage of U.S. Iran policy, but during 2018 and 2019, Trump's choices of John Bolton and Mike Pompeo for his top national security positions and their close collaboration with top Israeli officials had a profound impact on that policy, even taking the United States to the brink of war with Iran.

Supporting Israel's Region-wide Escalation

IN PREVIOUS YEARS, ISRAEL DEFENSE FORCES (IDF) had carried out dozens of attacks on what it had identified as convoys of missiles in Syria on their way to Lebanon for Hezbollah's arsenal, but it had also accepted certain implicit limits on those attacks, including their frequency, intensity and lethality. It had also foresworn any attack within Lebanon itself as risking the near-certainty of provoking retaliation by Hezbollah.[157] In mid-2017, however, the Netanyahu government laid the political groundwork for breaking those previously established "rules of the game" to carry out a major military escalation in Syria and even possible strikes in Lebanon. It began arguing that Iran was establishing permanent bases in Syria and secretly building factories in Syria and Lebanon for more precise missiles for Hezbollah's arsenal. Meanwhile, Israel was establishing its own long-term influence in Southern Syria, especially near the Israeli-occupied Golan Heights, by supporting anti-government Syrian armed groups.

The new escalation campaign was launched in February 2018 when a Syrian drone launched from the "T-4" Syrian government airbase near Palmyra with Iranian Quds Force advisers was shot down by an Israeli plane. The Israelis asserted that the drone had entered Israeli airspace armed with explosives, implying a rationale for relating, although the Israelis had long refused to observe any limitations on its own air operations in Syria.

The IDF then attacked the drone hanger at the T-4 base with fighter planes, one of which was shot down by Syrian anti-aircraft fire, thus going well beyond the "rules of the game" that had been observed by the two sides in previous years. And it went still further, immediately retaliating for the shoot-down of its plane by hitting the main Syrian army command-and-control bunker near Damascus and five Iranian communications facilities, killing several Iranian officers.

---

157. Amos Yadlin and Assaf Orion, "The Campaign between Wars: Faster, Higher, Fiercer?", Institute for National Security Studies, Insight No. 1209, August 30, 2019. https://www.inss.org.il/publication/the-campaign-between-wars-faster-higher-fiercer/

When Iran responded in March by bringing in a new anti-aircraft system to protect the T-4 base against further Israeli air attacks, the Israelis decided to go even further by destroying the system before it could be assembled, along with the hanger in which drones were stored. But Netanyahu faced a political problem: the U.S. government was divided over how to oppose Iranian presence in Syria and elsewhere, because the Pentagon was concerned that such an aggressive attack on Iranian personnel in Syria could result in U.S. troops being expelled from Iraq.[158]

The Israelis could have carried out the strike during late March or early April, but the Pentagon's objections could have caused political problems with the Trump administration. Fortunately for the Israelis, however, Trump's new choice for National Security Adviser, John Bolton, was to begin work on April 9, so the Israelis waited until April 9 to carry out the strike, which killed seven Iranian officers. The Israelis were obviously counting on Bolton's help in minimizing the impact of the Pentagon's opposition to the attack.[159]

The broader Israeli strategy was to escalate the attacks on Iranian personnel in Syria to the point where the Russians would have to intervene forcefully to put pressure on Iran to withdraw its personnel and proxy forces from Syria entirely. That strategy was only put into play, however, after the arrival of Bolton in the White House and Mike Pompeo as Secretary of State later in April. The entire leadership of the Washington Institute for Near East Policy (WINEP), whose function is to sell Israeli policies to Washington, explained in a July 2018 paper that Israel's attacks in Syria were designed to "present Russia with a dilemma: either reign in Iran's aggressive stance or face the possibility of a war between Israel, Iran and Hezbollah fought on Syrian territory...." To support that strategy, WINEP asked the Trump administration to "make clear to Israel, and Russia, that it has no objections to an active Israeli policy of preventing Iran from establishing a permanent military presence in Syria ."[160]

To achieve that objective, Israel was determined to get the Trump administration to reverse Trump's decision in March 2018 to withdraw U.S. troops from Syria by the end of the year. After Pompeo's arrival in Foggy Bottom, he quickly moved to accomplish that Israeli objective. In August he

---

158. Dion Nissenbaum and Rory Jones, "Israel Conferred with U.S. on Strike to Target Iranian War Gear," *Wall Street Journal*, April 12, 2018. https://www.wsj.com/articles/israel-conferred-with-u-s-on-strike-in-syria-to-target-iranian-war-gear-1524001066.
159. Nissenbaum and Jones, "Israel Conferred with U.S."
160. Katherine Bauer et al, *Toward a New U.S. Policy in Syria: Ground Zero for Countering Iran and Deterring an Islamic State Revival*, Washington Institute for Near East Policy, July 11, 2018, 3, 5.

appointed a senior WINEP official, Ambassador James F. Jeffrey, as the State Department's "special representative" for Syria with the task of developing a whole new U.S. Syria strategy.

In a July 2018 essay, the main strategic theorist of the new aggressive Israeli strategy, retired Brig. Gen. Assaf Orion, a former director of planning of the IDF general staff, hinted strongly at the importance of Bolton's and Pompeo's collaboration with Israeli strategy, noting the "coincidence of the U.S. withdrawal from JCPOA and Israel's clashes with Iran in Syria" and "the high level of coordination between the administration and the Israel government".[161]

By September 2018 Jeffrey was already telling the *Washington Post* that "the new policy is we're no longer pulling out by the end of the year" and that the U.S. troops in Syria would be used to "ensure an Iranian departure from Syria" as well as the defeat of ISIS. But the Pentagon was opposed to the draft policy, on the ground that it could be "the first step toward trying to provoke Iran into a military engagement."[162]

That, of course, was precisely what the Israelis were trying to do, and with the process of what the Netanyahu government believed was a reversal in U.S. Syria policy underway, the Israelis began a new, more provocative phase of their attacks in Syria. On September 18, Israeli warplanes hit a target in Latakia Province which Israeli intelligence suspected of being related to manufacture of more precise missiles. The target was close to a Russian airbase, and the attack prompted Syria to fire S-200 air defense missiles, which instead hit a Russian reconnaissance plane by mistake, killing Russian servicemen. Several days later, in a sharp rebuff to Israeli strategy, Russia announced it was providing its newer and more effective S-300 air defense system to the Syrian government.[163]

---

161. Assaf Orion, "The Response to Iranian Proxy War: Jerusalem's Power vs. the Quds Force," *Strategic Assessment*, 21/2 (July 2018), 34. https://www.inss.org.il/wp-content/uploads/2018/07/adkan21.2ENG_4-31-42.pdf

162. For an account of how Pompeo and Bolton sought to reverse Trump's Syria withdrawal policy on behalf of an Israeli strategy, see Gareth Porter, "How Trump Thwarted Calculated Israeli Effort to Keep U.S. in Syria," *The American Conservative*, January 14, 2019. https://www.theamericanconservative.com/articles/how-the-israeli-effort-to-keep-trump-in-syria-failed/

163. "Russia blames Israel after Syria downs plane while trying to repel attack," Times of Israel, September 18, 2018. https://www.timesofisrael.com/russia-blames-israel-after-syria-downs-plane-while-trying-to-repel-attack/; "Russia to give Syria S-300 air defense after accusations against Israel," Reuters, September 24, 2018. https://www.reuters.com/article/us-mideast-crisis-syria-russia/russia-to-give-syria-s-300-air-defense-after-accusations-against-israel-idUSKCN1M40ZA.

Jeffrey asserted again in early December that the U.S. military would remain in Syria until "the withdrawal of all Iranian-commanded forces from the entirety of Syria, and an irreversible political process" were achieved.[164] But no formal Presidential decision had been made to change Trump's previously enunciated policy, and on December 17, despite efforts by Netanyahu to sway his decision in two conversations with Trump and two with Pompeo, Trump declared publicly once again that all U.S. troops would be withdrawn from Syria.[165] The Israelis had relied on Bolton's informal control over the policy process, which turned out to be a poor substitute for presidential sign-off on a formal decision.

The maneuvering by Bolton in cooperation with Israel continued, however, in 2019, as he sought to preserve the small U.S. Special Forces enclave of Al Tank near the Syrian-Iraq border, from which the Israelis would keep the United States militarily involved in Syria against Iran and other Shiite militia forces. By Spring 2019, Bolton had prevailed on Trump to keep at least 200 U.S. troops at the base, along with 200 as advisers to Kurdish forces in Northern Syria.

Pushing Trump to the Brink of War

MEANWHILE, HOWEVER, BOLTON AND POMPEO WERE seeking to establish a new U.S. rationale for war with Iran based on phony claims of Iranian threats to Americans. After rockets were fired on the night of September 6, 2018 in Basra, Iraq and into Baghdad's "Green Zone" where foreign embassies are located, Bolton demanded and obtained options from the Pentagon for military retaliation against Iran in case any such incident were to harm U.S. diplomatic or military personnel in the future. And Pompeo used an article in *Foreign Affairs*, published in mid-October, to blame Iran and its "proxies" for the rockets and vow that the administration would "respond

164. "Briefing With Special Representative for Syria Engagement Ambassador James F. Jeffrey," December 3, 2018. https://www.state.gov/briefing-with-special-representative-for-syria-engagement-ambassador-james-f-jeffrey/
165. Barak Ravid, "Netanyahu asked Trump for a gradual pullout from Syria," *Axios*, December 31, 2018. https://www.axios.com/benjamin-netanyahu-donald-trump-syria-pullout-discussion-94610db1-bb1b-4faa-bd81-55e9ef4f517d.html.

swiftly and decisively in defense of American lives" if any such incident occurred in the future.[166]

The alleged threat Bolton and Pompeo had cooked up, however, was essentially a political ruse. The rockets fired in the vicinity of the Basra airport, where the U.S. consulate is also located, coincided with violent protests in Basra by anti-Iran protesters who had burned down the Iranian consulate and the offices of pro-Iranian political parties and militias there and even closed down Iran's only seaport that same day. And the one rocket fired into the Green Zone that same night was likely launched by anti-corruption protesters in Baghdad who had expressed their sympathy with the Basra protesters when it began weeks earlier and had previously tried to enter the Green Zone as a symbol of government authority. The Basra protesters, moreover, were violently opposed to pro-Iran parties and militias.[167]

Then, on May 5, 2019, Bolton issued a terse, one-paragraph statement announcing a sudden major increase in military tensions with Iran, accompanied by major changes in U.S. military deployments to the region. He claimed that the moves were a response to "troubling and escalatory indications and warnings" and that a Carrier Strike Group and a bomber task force were being sent to the region to "send an unmistakable message to the Iranian regime" that any attack on the United States "or . . . our allies" would be "met with unrelenting force."[168]

The Bolton declaration thus appeared to suggest the administration had obtained intelligence that Iran was preparing to carry out an attack against U.S. or allied targets. And Bolton had slipped into the statement an important codicil to the previous warnings he and Pompeo had voiced about a U.S.

---

166. Michael R. Pompeo, "Confronting Iran: The Trump Administration's Strategy," *Foreign Affairs*, November-December 2018. https://www.foreignaffairs.com/articles/middle-east/2018-10-15/michael-pompeo-secretary-of-state-on-confronting-iran; Eric Schmitt and Mark Landler, "Pentagon Officials Fear Bolton's Actions Increase Risk of Clash with Iran," *New York Times*, January 13, 2019. https://www.nytimes.com/2019/01/13/us/politics/bolton-iran-pentagon.html

167. On the Basra protests, including the shutdown of the seaport at Basra, see Jennifer Williams, "The violent protests in Iraq, explained," *Vox*, September 8, 2018. https://www.vox.com/world/2018/9/7/17831526/iraq-protests-basra-burning-government-buildings-iran-consulate-water. On the protests in Baghdad in July in sympathy with the weeks-long Basra protest, see "Baghdad joins southern anti-government protests," Rudaw News Service, Erbil, July 20, 2018. https://www.rudaw.net/english/middleeast/iraq/200720182.

168. "Statement from the National Security Advisor Ambassador John Bolton," May 5, 2019.https://www.whitehouse.gov/briefings-statements/statement-national-security-advisor-ambassador-john-bolton-2/. See Appendices, Document No.

"response" to any attack against Americans: now he was saying that U.S. retaliation with "unrelenting force" would be forthcoming if a "proxy" force allied to Iran were to attack a U.S. ally. That codicil opened up a plethora of new possible scenarios under which the administration could carry out an act of war against Iran.

The Bolton ploy came shortly after a meeting of the most senior U.S. and Israeli national security officials at the White House in April to discuss once again a common approach to "escalation scenarios" related to Iran, as reported by top Israeli journalist Barak Ravid, based on Israeli sources. At that meeting, Israel's Mossad had shared "scenarios" for possible Iranian moves that it had prepared, but no hard intelligence, according to Ravid's sources. A "senior Middle Eastern Intelligence official"—meaning a Mossad official—also told the *New York Times* in Jerusalem that Israeli intelligence had "warned U.S. officials" in recent weeks that "Iran or its proxies were planning to strike American targets in Iraq."[169]

Some news outlets carried sensational stories, based on leaks by officials in the State Department, NSC and CENTCOM pushing the new Iran scare on the intelligence supposedly showing Iranian threats to attack U.S. diplomatic facilities in Iraq or U.S. ships in the Gulf.[170] It was not long, however, before other sources in the Pentagon who thoroughly distrusted these claims revealed that Bolton and his allies had nothing more than politically motivated speculation to support their campaign. These claims were based on a directive said to have been issued by Iran's Supreme Leader Ali Khamenei to Iran's military forces, about which Bolton and Pompeo were deliberately misleading Congress and the public by omitting its crucial point, according to U.S officials who had seen the directive. The officials told the *Wall Street*

169. Barak Ravid, "Scoop: Israel passed White House intelligence on possible Iran plot," *Axios*, May 6, 2019. https://www.axios.com/israel-warned-trump-of-possible-iran-plot-bolton-34f25563-c3f3-41ee-a653-9d96b4541984.html; David M. Halbfinger, "Israel Presses the Case Against Iran, but Not for War," New York Times, May 16, 2019. https://www.nytimes.com/2019/05/16/world/middleeast/israel-iran-netanyahu-war.html.
170. See, for example, Courtney Kube, "US Officials: Iran Official Ok'd attacks on American military,' NBC News, May 9, 2019. https://www.nbcnews.com/news/military/u-s-officials-iran-official-ok-d-attacks-american-military-n1003421; Luis Martinez, "US photos showed cruise missiles on Iranian boats," ABC News, May 16, 2019. https://abcnews.go.com/Politics/us-photos-showed-anti-ship-missiles-iranian-boats/story?id=63076816.

Journal that the directive had actually said the forces "should prepare for possible attack by the U.S."[171]

Bolton's real objective in orchestrating that deception about an Iranian threat of attack was revealed a few days later when he directed acting Defense Secretary Patrick Shanahan to prepare a revised plan for a U.S. military response to any Iranian attack on American forces or advance beyond the JCPOA in regard to its nuclear program. At a White House meeting on May 9, Trump was presented with different options, the most serious of which was a plan to send 120,000 troops to the Persian Gulf region—nearly as many as were sent to invade Iraq in 2003.

But that Bolton move irritated Trump, who saw such planning for war as "getting ahead of his own thinking," according to a senior administration official. He was angry with both Bolton and Pompeo not only because they were trying to convince him to prepare for a military confrontation with Iran, but because of their broad hints that the real policy objective was regime change.[172]

In response to the series of escalatory anti-Iran moves orchestrated by Bolton and Pompeo, leaders in Tehran orchestrated their own signals to Washington that Iran would not passively accept U.S. efforts to shut down its economy. On May 12, four ships in the Sea of Oman near the Strait of Hormuz had small holes blown in them above the waterline by limpet mines, ensuring that there would be no danger to the ship or its personnel. Belgian journalist Elijah Magnier, who has access to senior IRGC officials, observed that the mostly symbolic sabotage of those ships "sends a clear message that no oil exports are possible if Iran will not be able to export its oil."[173]

On June 13 two more ships were similarly sabotaged with limpet mines in the Sea of Oman, sending the same message to the Trump administration. Bolton responded quickly by arranging for Pentagon announcement of the

---

171. Dion Nissenbaum, "U.S. Spent Two Weeks on Edge over Iran's Missile boats," *Wall Street Journal,* June 6, 2019. https://www.wsj.com/articles/u-s-spent-two-weeks-on-edge-over-irans-missile-boats-11559813523.

172. Eric Schmitt and Julian E. Barnes, "White House Reviews Military Plans Against Iran, in Echoes of Iraq War," *New York Times*, May 13, 2019. https://www.nytimes.com/2019/05/13/world/middleeast/us-military-plans-iran.html; John Hudson, Shane Harris, Josh Dawsey and Ann Gearan, "Trump purportedly frustrated by aides he believes are pushing him into war with Iran," *Washington Post* News Service. Stars and Stripes, May 15, 2016. https://www.stripes.com/news/us/trump-purportedly-frustrated-by-aides-he-believes-are-pushing-him-into-war-with-iran-1.581192

173. Elijah Magnier, "From Karbala to Al-Fujairah," May 13, 2019. https://ejmagnier.com/2019/05/13/from-karbala-to-al-fujairah-an-act-of-sabotage-may-end-prospects-of-a-summer-war-in-the-middle-east/.

dispatch of 1,000 more troops to the region, the day after Pompeo declared on "Face the Nation" June 16 that the administration was "considering a full range of options" to respond to the attacks, including the use of military force. But Trump sharply contradicted Pompeo's statement in an interview published two days later, effectively renouncing the option of a military attack on Iran in response to the limpet mine attacks, saying that what Iran had done was "so far...very minor".[174]

Then on June 20, Iran shot down a massive U.S. intelligence drone over the Strait of Hormuz, asserting that it was flying in Iran's airspace and had twice failed to heed a warning from the IRGC's air command. The U.S. Central Command claimed the drone was outside Iran's territorial waters but wouldn't answer reporters' questions. The Central Command and the Iranian military gave different sets of map coordinates for the location of the drone when it was shot down.[175]

Trump's account of the decision-making process was that he had authorized a strike against three targets involving Iranian radars, but that he changed his mind at the last minute and decided that the strike would cause too many casualties. A senior administration official told the *New York Times* that uncertainty about whether a U.S. aircraft had actually crossed into Iranian airspace was part of the reason he decided against the strikes.[176]

In private conversation the day after his decision against bombing three

---

174. Elana Johnson, "Trump prepares to bypass Congress to take on Iran," *Politico*, June 18, 2019. https://www.politico.com/story/2019/06/18/trump-congress-iran-1366756; "Exclusive: President Trump Calls Alleged Iranian Attack on Oil Tankers 'Very Minor'," *Time*, June 18, 2019. https://time.com/5608787/iran-oil-tanker-attack-very-minor/.

175. For Iran's account of the warnings, see Julian Borger, "How a Drone Flight took the U.S. and Iran to the Brink of War," *The Guardian*, June 21, 2019. https://www.theguardian.com/world/2019/jun/21/iran-latest-trump-drone-attack-timeline-airstrikes-called-off. For Iran's map coordinates and a map showing the entire alleged path of the drone, see Iranian Foreign Minister Zarif's tweets on June and 22. https://twitter.com/JZarif/status/1141772824086028288. On the initial CENTCOM reaction see Jackie Northam, "U.S and Iran Disagree Over Whether Drone Was Shot Down Over Iranian territory," *All Things Considered*, June 20, 2019. https://www.npr.org/programs/all-things-considered/2019/06/20/734344371. For the Pentagon's map coordinates. see "Pentagon releases map disputing claim US drone violated Iranian airspace," Fox News, June 20, 2019. https://www.foxnews.com/world/pentagon-releases-map-disputing-claim-us-drone-violated-iranian-airspace-irans-version-is-very-different.

176. Michael D. Shear, Helene Cooper and Eric Schmitt, "Trump Says He Was 'Cocked and Loaded' to Strike Iran, but Pulled Back," *New York Times*. June 21, 2019. https://www.nytimes.com/2019/06/21/us/politics/trump-iran-attack.html?module=inline.

Iranian radar emplacements, Trump said of the advisers who had urged him to retaliate against Iran, "These people want to push us into a war, and it's so disgusting."[177] During the short space of less than six weeks, Bolton had, with Pompeo's support, created a phony Iranian threat to attack U.S. interests, generated the option of the dispatch of tens of thousands of U.S. troops to the region in case of an alleged Iranian attack, and urged a U.S. attack on a military target in retaliation for the shutdown of a U.S. reconnaissance drone.[178]

Despite the tension between Trump and his advisers over their urging him to go to war, later in the summer the Israelis launched an even more aggressive series of drone strikes against Syria, Iraq and Lebanon, where Iran's ties with militia forces were strong. The IDF carried out a new series of attacks on bases, warehouses and other facilities belonging to Iran's allies in Iraq and Lebanon, beginning with a July 19 attack on an Iraqi militia base north of Baghdad and including at least three or four others in the next few weeks.

The Israelis claimed these attacks were necessary to prevent Iran and its allies from building factories for "precise weapons" for Hezbollah and from "attacking Israel with drones". But the July 19 attack was said to have destroyed a "cargo of guided missiles" without any indication that they represented such "precise weapons". And the Israeli attack on periphery of Iraq's Balad airbase August 22 caused an explosion of Katyusha rockets, mortar shell and grenades, suggesting it wasn't a depot for precision weapons at all.[179]

The Israelis also used a drone to bomb a target in the South Beirut neighborhood where Hezbollah's offices are located. Neither Israel nor Hezbollah had used military force across the Lebanon-Israel border since the 2006 war, so the Israeli drone attack violated what both sides understood to be an "unwritten understanding" about the "rules of the game" and was recognized by Israeli strategists to be a highly provocative move.[180] The target was said

177. Michael C. Bender and Gordon Lubold, "Trump Bucked National Security Advisers on Proposed Iran Attack," *Wall Street Journal*, June 23, 2019. https://www.wsj.com/articles/trump-bucked-national-security-aides-on-proposed-iran-attack-11561248602.
178. David M. Halbfinger, Ben Hubbard and Ronen Bergman, "The Israel-Iran Shadow War Escalates and Breaks Into the Open," *New York Times*, August 28, 2019. https://www.nytimes.com/2019/08/28/world/middleeast/israel-iran-shadow-war.html
179. Alissa J. Rubin and Ronen Bergman, "Israeli Airstrike Hits Weapons Depot in Iraq," *New York Times*, August 22, 2019. https://www.nytimes.com/2019/08/22/world/middleeast/israel-iraq-iran-airstrike.html?module=inline.
180. Amos Yadlin and Assaf Orion, "The Campaign between Wars: Faster, Higher Fiercer?" INSS Insight No. 1209, August 30, 2019, pp. 1-3. https://www.inss.org.il/wp-content/uploads/2019/08/No.-1209.pdf.

to be a "planetary mixer", which could be used to improve the efficiency of a missile's engine as well as its accuracy.[181]

Even assuming that Iran and/or Hezbollah were attempting to install factories for more accurate weapons for Hezbollah in Lebanon, these Israeli attacks were not an effort to keep peace in the region by strengthening deterrence. They were based an official IDF doctrine of "campaign between wars" in regard to Lebanon that does not accept any such norms. "The IDF does not hide the fact that it is preparing for war in Lebanon," Udi Dekel and Assaf Orion, both retired IDF generals who had formerly been in charge of planning for the general staff, wrote in 2017.[182] The Israelis also do not deny that Hezbollah's missile arsenal is the for the purpose of deterring attack by Israel, not for preparing to initiate a future war. [183] The IDF believed, however, that there was not a "high risk of war" in carrying out the strikes, because Hezbollah and Iran both still prefer to avoid "broad escalation", according to the two former senior IDF officials.[184]

The Israelis also know that Iran's policy in building and improving Hezbollah's arsenal is aimed at deterring Israel from attacking Iran as well. As retired IDF general Assaf Orion acknowledged in an interview in September 2019, Iran regards its own ballistic missile deterrent as inadequate, and arming Hezbollah is a way for Iran to compensate for that weakness. "For the same amount of money," he observed, "you can produce one missile in Iran or a thousand in Lebanon."[185]

The Israeli decisions to launch unprecedented strikes on targets in Syria, Iraq and Lebanon were clearly related to what had happened within the Trump administration. By late August, the hope that Pompeo and Bolton could trap Trump into a retaliatory blow against Iran had been unexpectedly disappointed. And in its place was an Israeli fear that Trump wanted

---

181. Amos Harel, "Beirut Strike Target: Vital Iranian Device for Hezbollah's Mass Missile Production," *Haaretz*, August 29, 2019. https://www.haaretz.com/middle-east-news/.premium-israel-hezbollah-strike-beirut-lebanon-iran-precision-missile-1.7761938
182. Udi Dekel and Assaf Orion, "The Next War against Hezbollah: Strategic and Operational Considerations," in Udi Dekel, Gabi Siboni and Omer Einav, eds., *The Quiet Decade: In the Aftermath of the Second Lebanon War*, 2006-2016, Institute for National Security Studies memorandum 167, July 2017, p. 131. http://www.inss.org.il/wp-content/uploads/2017/07/memo167_6.pdf.
183. Carmit Valensi and Yoram Schweitzer, "Hezbollah's Concept of Deterrence According to Nasrallah: From the Second Lebanon War to the Present," in *The Quiet Decade*, pp. 115-126.
184. Yadlin and Orion, "The Campaign between Wars," p. 3.
185. Gareth Porter interview with Assaf Orion, September 4, 2019.

to negotiate with Iran, and even to soften the sanctions temporarily for that purpose. Former senior IDF officials Amos Yadlin and Assaf Orion observed that there were "hints of possible budding negotiations between the United States and Iran on the nuclear file, which are not to the Israeli Prime Minister's liking." They suggested that the Israeli offensive, including the strike in the Beirut suburb, was not only to hit "enemy capabilities" but to "prod them into a hasty response that might compromise the chances of a dialogue opening between Iran and the United States."[186]

The IDF fully expected that the drone strike against a target in Hezbollah's stronghold south of Beirut August 25 would result in a Hezbollah retaliatory strike. And Netanyahu certainly hoped that the such a retaliation by Hezbollah could be used by Bolton and Pompeo to argue that the United States should respond militarily as they had both asserted. The new Bolton codicil to the previous Bolton-Pompeo warnings that the United States would retaliate for any attack against a U.S. ally—even by a "proxy" of Iran—remained in place.

Pompeo pushed the idea that the Israeli strikes—including the one in south Beirut—were for Israel's defense against an Iranian threat. On August 25, after a telephone conversation with Netanyahu, a statement from Pompeo's office said, "The secretary expressed support for Israel's right to defend itself against threats posed by the Iranian [Islamic] Revolutionary Guard Corps and to take action to prevent imminent attacks against Israeli assets in the region."[187]

But Trump had no interest in hyping the threat to Israel or promising to respond to the expected Hezbollah retaliation. When Hezbollah did retaliate on September 1 by firing an anti-tank missile at an Israeli armored car across the border, apparently wounding IDF personnel inside, the Israeli press was told that there were no casualties, and that the IDF had deliberately misled Hezbollah to believe otherwise.[188] Recognizing that Trump had no interest in getting involved, the Israelis made no threat of further retaliation.

Trump's relationship with Bolton, moreover, had become extremely tense

186. Amos Yadlin and Assaf Orion, "The Campaign between Wars: Faster, Higher, Fiercer?" Institute for National Security Studies, INSS Insight no. 1209, August 30, 2019. https://www.inss.org.il/publication/the-campaign-between-wars-faster-higher-fiercer/.

187. "Pompeo speaks with Netanyahu on Iran, backs Israel's preemptive raid," *Times of Israel*, August 25, 2019. https://www.timesofisrael.com/pompeo-powwows-with-netanyahu-on-iran-backs-israels-preemptive-raid/.

188. "Reports: Hezbollah missiles narrowly missed armored car with 5 soldiers inside," *Times of Israel*, September 3, 2009. https://www.timesofisrael.com/reports-hezbollah-nearly-missed-manned-armored-car-driving-in-breach-of-orders/.

over the issue of holding talks with Iran. On September 9, Bolton clashed with Trump over the President's suggestion that he might be willing to ease U.S. sanctions sufficiently to hold talks with Iran, beginning with a possible meeting with President Rouhani at the United Nations.[189] Whether it was Bolton or Trump who raised the issue of a Bolton resignation first is unclear, but Trump announced his resignation in a tweet the following day.

Trump had again frustrated Netanyahu's hopes for an escalation of the U.S.-Iran conflict into a military confrontation. But the underlying mechanism of U.S.-Iran war crisis remained intact in the form of the Trump administration's sanctions policy aimed explicitly at preventing Iran from exporting its oil and demanding that it give up its right to self-defense. And Pompeo, who was equally or even more committed to confrontation with Iran, remained in place and likely to do whatever he could to discourage a sharp change in policy toward Iran.

---

189. Jennifer Jacobs, Saleha Mohsin, Jenny Leonard, and David Wainer, "Trump Discussed Easing Iran Sanctions, Prompting Bolton Pushback," *Bloomberg*, September 11, 2019. https://www.bloomberg.com/news/articles/2019-09-11/trump-rouhani-meeting-odds-improve-after-john-bolton-s-exit.

6. Can Trump Avoid War with Iran?

T HE THREAT OF WAR HANGS OVER the U.S.-Iran conflict because of the Trump administration's reimposition of the sanctions that were removed under the JCPOA. That policy has been made even more aggressive and draconian by a "maximum pressure" campaign that has as its objective forcing Iran to bow to demands that violate its rights as a sovereign state. The means it employs, moreover, are the economic equivalent to an act of war against Iran, because it has exactly the same effect as a naval blockade. The sanctions are a frontal attack on Iran's inherent right as a sovereign state to participate in the global trade system.

Beyond that elemental act of aggression against Iran, the Trump administration's strategy also seeks to deprive Iran of the sovereign right of self-defense, which obviously includes the right to maintain the normal means of deterrence and defense through retaliatory capabilities in the form of ballistic missiles. In the modern world system of international politics, that objective is tantamount to denying Iran's right to exist. The Trump administration has masked the reality of that double-barreled aggression against Iran by putting out a torrent of crude propaganda about alleged Iranian "destabilization" and "terrorism", none of which is supported by actual fact.

A precedent for such demand for a state to give up its right to defend itself was set by the treatment of Saddam Hussein's Iraq after the first Gulf War. But the circumstances surrounding the cases could hardly be more starkly different. In the case of Iraq, the United States had already defeated Saddam's forces and imposed a highly unequal relationship in which the U.S. was confident that it could use force to take down the regime. In the case of Iran, however, the capability to resist a U.S. attack has not only survived the U.S. economic war but has continued to develop over the past decade. In fact, Iran now has capability to impose costs on the United States and its allies that are greater than any state that Washington has ever sought to dominate through the Cold War or after.

Therein lies a new crisis in U.S. foreign policy, which now demands that the political system and the national security state face squarely the reality that the U.S.'s unrealistic demands on Iran, along with the U.S. assault on Iran's right to trade, which is absolutely unacceptable to Iran, pose a threat of war with Iran that would be the ultimate disaster in a long sequence of disastrous Middle East policy decisions going all the way back to the Bill Clinton administration. There is a desperate need for fundamental change in Iran policy, but it is not clear from where the impetus for change could come.

Legal Chicanery and the "Maximum Pressure" Campaign

THE FUNDAMENTAL TOOL THAT HAS BEEN key to the U.S. attack on the Iranian economy did not begin with Trump administration. That tool is the application of "extraterritorial sanctions"—sanctions based on the application of U.S. law to punish someone beyond U.S. legal jurisdiction to coerce Iran's erstwhile trade and investment partners around the world to cut off those economic relationships—and especially to stop importing Iranian oil. That policy tool exploits the global financial power of the United States based on the dominance of the U.S. dollar in world trade. The dollar's role as the main reserve currency allows the United States to compel foreign companies to abide by U.S. policies toward Iran. The U.S. leverage lies in the fear of those foreign companies of being barred from participation in economic transactions involving the U.S. financial system.

The United States had begun using such extraterritorial sanctions to reduce foreign trade with and investment in Iran during the Obama administration, following the passage of UN Security Council resolution 1929 in June 2010. That resolution banned all Iranian enrichment activities and ballistic missile development. But even more important, Undersecretary of the Treasury for Terrorism and Financial Intelligence Stuart Levey, who was leading the U.S. effort to cripple the Iranian economy, had ensured that language was included in the resolution that could be used to intimidate

any foreign company doing business with Iran. The crucial language in resolution 1929 calls upon all states to "prevent the provision of financial services, including insurance or re-insurance" or any "assets or resources" to
any Iranian entity if the states have "information that provides reasonable
grounds to believe that such services, assets or resources could contribute to
Iran's proliferation-sensitive nuclear activities, or the development of nuclear weapon delivery systems...."[190]

In Congressional testimony, Levey revealed the hidden legal agenda
behind that language. "The vast body of public information demonstrating
the scope of Iran's illicit conduct and deceptive practices—practices that
have facilitated its proliferation activities," Levey declared, "makes it nearly
impossible for financial institutions and governments to assure themselves
that transactions with Iran could not contribute to proliferation-sensitive
activities." In another speech, Levey was more explicit. "[T]he operating pre-
sumption," he said, "should be that virtually all transactions or financial services involving Iran could contribute to its nuclear or missile programs."[191]

Based on this legal chicanery, Levey's Treasury Department hoped to
exploit the fear of foreign companies doing business with Iran that they
would stand to be accused of having aided and abetted Iranian nuclear or
missile activities, which the Obama administration had now criminalized.
The European Union also adopted an aggressive program of sanctions based
on the same legal premise.[192] Very quickly, major European banks and cor-
porations, frightened by the prospect of being linked to Iran's supposed drive
for nuclear weapons, began to pull out of trade and investment in Iran and
refused to deal with its banks and companies, and the Iranian economy went
into a tailspin.

Levey's clever ploy delighted Israel and the pro-Israel political forces in
Washington. But to the chagrin of the Israeli government and its supporters in Washington, Obama then negotiated the JCPOA with Iran, which
included an end to the potentially crippling sanctions that Levey had been
engineering. Once Trump had pulled out of the nuclear deal in 2018, however, the scene was set for an even more aggressive and expansive scheme
to use extraterritorial sanctions against Iran began to unfold. In March

---

190. United Nations Security Council resolution 1929, June 9, 2010, paragraph 21.
See Document No. 6 in the Appendices to this book.
191. Written Testimony by Under Secretary for Terrorism and Financial Intelligence
Stuart Levey Before the House Committee on Foreign Affairs, December 1, 2010;
Remarks by Stuart Levey at the Center for Strategic and International Studies,
September 20, 2010. .
192. Remarks by Stuart Levey at CSIS, September 20, 2010.

2019, Pompeo, with Bolton's support, pushed for designating Iran's Islamic Revolutionary Guard Corps, which is, in effect, Iran's main military organization, as a terrorist organization. The White House announced on April 8 that the United States was designating the IRGC as a terrorist group.

It was a step that puzzled observers in Washington, because both the Pentagon and the CIA had long opposed such a designation as setting a precedent for other countries designating the U.S. military as terrorists and also risked the Iraqi government retaliating by expelling U.S. forces.[193] Furthermore, the IRGC had already been designated by Treasury in October 2017 for activities that "assist in, sponsor, or provide financial, material, or technological support for, or financial or other services to or in support of" the IRGC "Quds Force", which is the foreign operations arm of the IRGC.[194]

The new Treasury move was merely another scheme to broaden even further the scope of financial sanctions against foreign firms dealing with Iran. As Mark Dubowitz, the CEO of the Foundation for the Defense of Democracies, who was the first and primary political proponent of the move, explained to *The Atlantic*, it would "deter more business and diminish current business that's still going on between the Europeans and Iranians, and the Asians and the Iranians."[195]

Dubowitz was referring to the fact that the designation would allow the United States to extend its criminal jurisdiction to any foreign company doing business with Iran, because the issue would now fall under U.S. criminal statute relating to terrorism. It would use the same argument that the Obama administration's Treasury Department had used to intimidate businesses—that so much of Iran's economy was controlled by the IRGC that the U.S. presumes that any financial transaction with Iran would benefit the IRGC and thus contribute to its alleged terrorist objectives. But now

---

193. Edward Wong and Eric Schmitt, "U.S. Pressures Iraq Over Embrace of Militias Linked to Iran," *New York Times*, March 19, 2019. https://www.nytimes.com/2019/03/19/world/middleeast/iraq-us-tensions-iran.html#click=https://t.co/QpghDjoMF3

194. Department of the Treasury press release, "Treasury Designates the IRGC under Terrorism Authority and Targets IRGC and Military Supporters under Counter-Proliferation Authority," October 13, 2017. https://www.treasury.gov/press-center/press-releases/Pages/sm0177.aspx.

195. Kathy Gilsinan, "The U.S. Escalates Even Further Against Iran—To What End?" *The Atlantic*, April 8, 2018. https://www.theatlantic.com/politics/archive/2019/04/trump-iran-revolutionary-guard-terrorist-organization/586663/. Dubowitz first advocated the IRGC designation as a terrorist organization in Mark Dubowitz and Ray Takeyh, "Labeling Iran's Revolutionary Guard," *Foreign Affairs*, March 6, 2017. https://www.foreignaffairs.com/articles/iran/2017-03-06/labeling-irans-revolutionary-guard.

the Trump administration could threaten not only to use its financial clout against any foreign company doing business with Iran but to threaten them with criminal prosecution over a trumped-up charge of supporting Iranian "terrorism."

The main targets of the new terrorism-related sanctions would be foreign companies selling oil to Iran. Pompeo, who was deeply involved in the sanctions policy, focused on the objective of essential eliminating Iran's oil export earnings, which accounted for more than 70 percent of its export income. On April 21, 2019, Pompeo announced that the waivers on eight oil importing countries that had been granted temporarily in October 2017 would be terminated. The eight countries, led by China and India, each of which accounted for a third of the total, provided $50 billion in annual export earnings for Iran. "[W]e're going to zero across the board," Pompeo declared.[196]

But the administration's plan went much further. Contrary to its propaganda line that the sanctions were only aimed at the regime itself and not ordinary Iranians, for whom it professed only the warmest friendship, and that food and medicine were exempt from the U.S. sanctions against Iran, the administration's Iran sanctions strategy was aimed precisely at imposing the maximum possible hardship on the rest of the population.

Clearly reflecting that aim, in October 2018, the Treasury Department targeted the Parsian Bank, the biggest non-state bank in Iran, for sanctions. Some European banks had already begun to refuse to process payments even from Iranian firms that were exempt from sanctions, because of fear of U.S. penalties, but Parsian Bank had earned the trust of European companies and banks for being responsible and free of ties with the Iranian government.[197]

Treasury's explanation for its targeting Parsian Bank reveals how specious its rationale had become. It said that an investment company that had put money from the Iran Zinc Mines Development Company (IZMDC), Iran's leading zinc and lead mining and processing company, into Parsian Bank was part of a chain of financial links involving five separate business organizations that ultimately led to one allegedly owned by the Basij, the Iranian paramilitary organization. The Basij is in turn allied with the Islamic

---

196. "U.S. to end all waivers on imports of Iranian oil, crude price jumps," *Reuters*, April 21, 2019.
197. Erin Cunningham, "Fresh sanctions on Iran are already choking off medicine imports, economists say," *Washington Post*, November 17, 2018.

Revolutionary Guard Corps.[198] The designation of Parsian Bank was based on a bank having a deposit from an investment company with seven degrees of separation from the IRGC, which had been declared a terrorist group a few months earlier solely in order to get at Iranian financial institutions that had nothing to do with it.

The dishonest methodology used to justify the designation of Parsian Bank, moreover, was a departure from past Treasury Department practice, which had required a direct relationship of ownership by a designated institution, according to sanctions lawyer Tyler Cullis. But Cullis pointed out that U.S. prosecutors "have discretion to determine who or what constitutes 'IRGC'," as was demonstrated when the Justice Department sought the seizure and forfeiture of the Grace 1 Iranian oil tanker in August 2019, on the ground that it was an IRGC "asset"—simply by the convenient assertion that IRGC exercises control over the entire Iranian economy. As Cullis observed, the Trump administration had effectively "criminalized the Iranian economy."

After Treasury had targeted Parsian Bank, Iranian Foreign Minister Mohammad Javad Zarif posted letters from four European pharmaceutical companies announcing that they were terminating all business activities in Iran. In a coldly cynical verbal shrug, Brian Hook, the U.S. "Special Representative for Iran", told reporters, "The burden is not on the United States to identify the safe channels" for humanitarian trade.[199]

Along with much higher prices for food and medicines manufactured in Iran, because of the precipitous drop in imports, the deliberate decision by Treasury to go after the main Iranian bank handling such transactions created an acute shortage of drugs needed for life-saving treatments, especially for chemotherapy for cancer patients, which were imported from Europe.[200]

By October 2019, however, the World Bank and the IMF had estimated the contraction of the Iranian economy in 2019 at 8.7 percent and 9.5 percent, respectively. Price inflation in food and fuel, the two items with the greatest impact on the population, was estimated to be as high as 63.5 percent, according to the Statistical Center of Iran.[201] The IMF described

---

198. Department of the Treasury, "Treasury Sanctions Vast Financial Network Supporting Iranian Paramilitary Force That Recruits and Trains Child Soldiers," October 16, 2018.
199. Cunningham, "Fresh sanctions on Iran."
200. Abbas Kebriaeezadeh, "U.S. Sanctions are Killing Cancer Patients in Iran," *Foreign Policy*, August 14, 2019.
201. "Iran economy to shrink 9.5 percent this year amid tougher U.S. sanctions, says IMF," *Reuters*, October 15, 2019; "Iran's economy plummets under weight of sanctions," DW, October 23, 2019._

the impact on the Iranian economy and society as "severe distress".[202] But any notion that the U.S. "Maximum Pressure" strategy would cause the Iran public to oppose its government's policies should have been shattered by a survey of Iranian opinion in October 2019. The survey carried out on 1,000 Iranians by researchers at the University of Maryland showed that four in five Iranian express negative attitudes toward the United States and support the Iranian military role in Syria and that three in five support its ballistic missile program as a deterrent to attack on Iran. A solid majority of Iranians, moreover, now question whether Iran should have signed the nuclear deal in the first place, because of the failure of the United States and European allies to deliver on their economic commitments under the agreement.[203]

The problem posed by the U.S. "Maximum Pressure" campaign, therefore, is that it has already driven Iranian public opinion very far away from the more moderate position of the government of President Rouhani and Foreign Affairs minister Zarif to a position aligned with the viewpoint of the Islamic Revolutionary Guard Corps and the conservative nationalists that Iran should not have negotiated on its nuclear program to begin with, and that it should continue to defend its interests in the region in the face of U.S. pressures. The shift in Iranian public opinion does not offer any room for the present government—and the Supreme Leader Ali Khamenei—to maneuver diplomatically.

Instead, it creates obvious pressure on the government to take a very hard line toward the Trump administration's assault on Iran's right to trade.

In his speech before the United Nations General Assembly in September 2019, Rouhani called U.S. sanctions "a form of economic terrorism and a breach of the 'Right to Development'". He refrained from making any threat to retaliate or to use force in response to these sanctions, but that restraint did not necessarily reflect Iran's strategic plan for resisting the ruthless U.S. economic pressures on the country's economy. The Iranian strategic calculus is more fully reflected in the combination of declaratory threats by the Iranian military to close the Strait of Hormuz if Iran is denied the right to export its oil, and the demonstration of readiness to act on the threat carried

---

202. Najmeh Bozorgmehr, "Iran suffering 'severe distress' from US sanctions, says IMF," *Financial Times*, October 17, 2019.

203. Nancy Gallagher, Ebrahim Mohsani and Clay Ramsay, "Iranian Pubic Own under 'Maximum Pressure," Center for International and Security Studies at Maryland, School of Public Policy, University of Maryland, October 2019. https://cissm.umd.edu/sites/default/files/2019-10/Iranian%20PO%20under%20Maximum%20Pressure_101819_full.pdf

out in Spring 2019 and the demonstration of the capability to strike U.S. targets in the region during the year.

Those demonstrations of Iran's power in 2019 showed that if and when a U.S.-Iranian confrontation over sanctions comes, Iran will be capable of imposing far more costs on the United States in the event of war than only a few short years ago. And therein lies a fundamental change in the dynamics of the U.S.-Iran confrontation.

The New Persian Gulf Military Balance

INTO THE SECOND DECADE OF THE 21st century, the U.S. military had counted on its ability to destroy both Iran's surface ships and its shore-based anti-ship missiles in any confrontation over the Strait of Hormuz. But as Iran's anti-ship missile capabilities continued to increase over the past decade, the original assumption the U.S. Navy could do the job from within the Strait itself was increasingly called into question.

So, when the U.S.S. Abraham Lincoln carrier strike group was sent to the area in May 2019 as a symbolic show of force in response to the alleged increase in threat from Iran, the carrier and its warships stayed out of the Strait of Hormuz. Instead it carried out joint exercises in the North Arabian Sea 600 miles away. Rear Adm. Michael E. Boyle, the commander of the carrier strike group, explained to the *New York Times* that U.S. planes could still strike Iran from there, but, "They can reach us when we're there. When we're here, they can't."[204]

That observation highlighted one of the key shifts in the military balance between the United States and Iran that had occurred over the previous decade. But the shift in military balance between the United States and Iran had gone even further. New Iranian weapons unveiled in 2019 and two incidents involving the shoot-down of an expensive U.S. drone and the attack on Saudi Arabia's most important oil facility had revealed the new Iranian capabilities that made clear Iran's ability to reach U.S. military targets anywhere in the Gulf region, along with those of American allies.

Iran's most important advances in military technology have been in developing cruise missiles and drones. An analyst from the hardline anti-Iran

---

204. Helene Cooper, "This U.S. Warship Threatens Iran (From 600 Miles Away)," *New York Times*, August 23, 2019. https://www.nytimes.com/2019/08/23/us/politics/warship-iran.html.

Foundation for the Defense of Democracies even suggested that Iran is an incipient "drone superpower".[205] And some of its drones are also cruise missiles that can be steered remotely. Iran's cruise missiles include the Hoveyzeh, unveiled by the IRGC in February 2019. It is a surface-to-surface cruise missile with a range of 1,350 km (728 n.m.), which would expose the full range of U.S. bases and other high-value targets in the region vulnerable to a ground-hugging missile for which U.S.-made electronic defenses are not effective.[206]

Another important addition to Iran's military capabilities is the Bavar-373 anti-aircraft defense system. It is not simply a knock-off or variant of the Russian S-300, which Russia finally provided to Iran in 2015, because Iran began developing its own system in 2011, after Russia had refused to give the S-300 to Iran the previous year. And because it is an indigenous system, the Bavar-373 is both better adapted to Iran's specific military needs and more difficult for the United States to counter than the S-300, which has now been adopted by several countries with ties to the United States. The new Iranian system, which can engage dozens of incoming aircraft or missiles simultaneously at ranges up 200 km, is closer to Russia's S-400 than the S-300 in its effectiveness, as its name is intended to suggest.[207]

The weapons that were in the spotlight in 2019, however, were two longer-range drone systems introduced publicly by Iran's Houthi allies in Yemen in July 2019 but clearly based on original Iranian designs. The United Nations Panel of Experts on Yemen had examined a previously unknown Houthi drone/cruise missile in 2018 that had been captured by Saudi-supported forces in Yemen and that panel called "UAV-X". It had a more powerful rear-mounted engine that the panel said would give it a range of between 1,200 and 1,500 km. That description fit the Quds-1 introduced by the Houthis in July. The Samad-3, also shown in the Houthi introduction to its family of drones, had a "conformal fuel tank" on top of the body, which would give it a range of 1,500-1,700 km, according to the Yemeni Army.[208]

The new long-range drone capabilities of the Houthis and of Iran were dramatically revealed on September 14, 2019, when a combination of drones and cruise missiles hit Saudi Arabia's most important oil export complex at

---

205. Seth J. Frantzman, "Iran is becoming a drone superpower," *The Hill*, July 19, 2019.

206. Jeremy Binnie, "Iran unveils new long-range cruise missile," *Janes 360*, February 4, 2019.

207. The most complete technical analysis of the Bavar-373, including a systematic comparison with the S-300, see "Iran's Bavar-373: A Profile," Iran GeoMil, August 24, 2019.

208. Final report of the Panel of Experts on Yemen, January 25, 2019, UN document S/2019/83, p. 30; "Houthis' New Missiles & Combat Drones," South Front, July 7, 2019.

Abqaiq/Khurais, including the largest oil stabilization plant in the world. On September 14, 2019, it was struck with a combination of drones and cruise missiles that hit precisely the structures in the complex necessary to cut Saudi oil production from 9.8 to 4.1 million barrels of oil a day and forced the shutdown of the complex for an unknown period.

The Houthis (officially "Ansar Allah") said they had launched 10 drones of three different types from three different locations in Yemen at the facility. The Trump Administration insisted that there was no evidence the drones and cruise missiles came from Yemen, and that it was beyond the Houthis capabilities. In fact, however, the Houthis had demonstrated on May 14, 2019 that their drones could reach that far with accuracy, when seven Houthi drones hit two Saudi pumping stations on the East-West oil pipeline, forcing the government to temporarily shut them down.[209]

Nevertheless, the September 14 attack underlined the reality that U.S. bases as well as other military and economic targets all across the Middle East could now be hit with pinpoint precision by Iran. Lest the point be missed in the focus on the shocking nature of the attack to a key oil facility, the head of IRGC Aerospace Forces, Amirali Hajjadeh, immediately declared, without referring explicitly to the attack, "Everybody should know that all American bases and their aircraft carriers in a distance up to 2,000 kilometers are within range of our missiles."[210] And that was only part of the new reality. The Pentagon had also lost the strategic advantage over Iran it had enjoyed for many years from the fact that Iranian missiles were simply too inaccurate to do any serious damage to U.S. bases in the region.[211]

Even as late as July 2019, the Pentagon sent 500 more troops and additional Patriot anti-missile batteries to Saudi Arabia as part of an agreement for the United States to reoccupy Prince Sultan Airbase near Riyadh to strengthen U.S. "deterrence" of Iran.[212] But the Abqaiq attack showed that

---

209. Vivian Yee, "Yemen's Houthi Rebels Attack Saudi Oil Facilities, Escalating Tensions in Gulf," *New York Times*, May 14, 2019. Neither the Times story nor coverage by AP and AFP noted the key point that the attack proved the Houthis had the capability to strike the heart of Northern Saudi Arabia, hundreds of miles from Yemen.

210. "Iran: U.S. bases, aircraft carriers within range of our missiles," *Reuters*, Ynet News, September 15, 2019. https://www.ynetnews.com/articles/0,7340,L-5588944,00.html

211. Jacob Heim, "The Iranian Missile Threat to Air Bases," *Air and Space Power Journal*, v. 29, no. 4, July-Aug. 2015, pp. 27-50.

212. Courtney Kube, "U.S. military has begun reestablishing an airbase inside Saudi Arabia," NBC News, July 19, 2019.

the Patriot system, on which both Saudi Arabia and UAE have depended for missile defense, couldn't cope with either Iranian drones or cruise missiles.[213]

The Saudi oil facility strike was not the first time that the United States had been taken by surprise by the newly-developed Iranian missile capabilities. Until June 21, 2019, the Pentagon had been confident that the $220 million U.S. drone—its newest and most expensive aircraft—was not vulnerable to any Iranian air defense system.[214] After the June 21 shoot-down, a Pentagon official told Newsweek that U.S. officials believed that Iran must have used a Russian S-125 Neva/Pechora surface-to-air missile system, which has a range of only 17 km.[215]

But in fact Iran had hit the U.S. drone with its indigenously produced "Third of Khordad" medium-range air defense system with a 200 km range.[216] According to an IRGC general who spoke with journalist Elijah J. Magnier, it was a modified version of what was originally the SA-6 Soviet surface-to-air missile, the development of which began in 2013, after the Russians had declined to provide the latest version of that missile.[217]

The strike on Saudi Arabia's most important oil facility presumably could not have happened without joint Iranian-Houthi planning. So, it was both a decisive Houthi signal to Saudi Arabia to end its war in Yemen and an Iranian signal to the United States that it had the military capabilities with which to resist U.S. pressure.

Can Trump Avoid War with Iran?

IN THE AFTERMATH OF THE STRIKE on the Saudi oil facility, the U.S. political and policymaking systems were thrown into a state of flux, in which the

---

213. Stephen Kaylin and Sylvia Westall, "Costly Saudi defenses prove no match for drones, cruise missiles," *Reuters*, September 17, 2019.

214. Sebastian Roblin, "A War Begins? How Iran Shot Down a U.S. RQ4N Surveillance Drone BAMS-D," *The National Interest*, June 21, 2019.

215. James LaPorta and Tom O'Connor, "Donald Trump Decided to Strike Iranian Missile System, Then Changed His Mind," *Newsweek*, June 21, 2019. Technical specifications of the Russian system are from Carlo Kopp, "Technical Report APA-TR-2009-0602," July 2012, *Air Power Australia*, January 27, 2014.

216. "Iran's Raad (3rd Khordad) Long Range Missile System Responsible For Downing $220 Million American Drone," *Military Watch Magazine*, June 21, 2019.

217. Elijah J. Magnier, "How Iran Decided to Down a U.S. Drone and Narrowly Averted War by Sparing Another U.S. Plane," June 23, 2019.

assumptions that had long guided policy toward Iran were suddenly in question. To begin with, the calculation that had informed the Trump administration's "Maximum Pressure" policy was that Iran would have to give way because Iran could not risk war with the United States. As one U.S. official told *Washington Post* columnist David Ignatius, it had turned out that Iran was "much more risk-tolerant than American analysts had believed."[218]

Trump obviously wants to avoid war with Iran. Even as Bolton and Pompeo were trying to engineer a military confrontation in early May, Trump had begun to make it clear privately to aides that he was not interested in threatening, much less carrying out a military retaliation for an Iranian use of force that did not directly affect U.S. personnel or assets. He didn't even ask the Pentagon for military options to respond to the Saudi attack but reverted instead to his previously expressed interest in making a new diplomatic deal with Iran.[219] Trump's desire to avoid war was rooted, moreover, in a political calculation in anticipation of a presidential election year: he believed his political base was tired of U.S. wars and wanted out of the Middle East.

But a war with Iran would result not from a U.S. retaliation for a minor incident, but from the Iranian response to the provocation inherent in the Trump administration's assault on the Iranian economy: it would be triggered by an Iranian move to close the Strait of Hormuz, which senior officials of the IRGC have warned in the past would happen if Iran were denied its right to export its oil. On the eve of the announcement by Pompeo that there would be no waivers, the IRGC Naval forces commander Alireza Tangsiri had declared, "If we are prevented from using it, we will close it."[220] The new generation of more advanced military capabilities that Iran has developed over the past decade and the two incidents that took the United States and its allies by surprise have given new credibility to that Iranian threat.

Iran would most likely shut down the Strait of Hormuz to oil traffic by dropping thousands of mines in the Strait with hundreds of small military and civilian boats, while warning the U.S. military not to bring U.S. ships into the Strait to clear them. The U.S. war plan for the Strait, however, has long called for to sending in minesweepers to try to clear the Strait over a period of days to weeks. Iran would then be likely to hit at least one minesweeper

---

218. David Ignatius, "Trump's conflict with Iran is a crisis of his own making," *Omaha World Herald*, September 22, 2019.
219. On Dunford's statement that Trump had not requested military options, see David Martin, CBS News, September 18, 2019.
220. "Iran to block Strait of Hormuz if its benefits denied: IRGC Navy cmdr.," *Mehr News Agency*, April 22, 2018. https://en.mehrnews.com/news/144384/Iran-to-block-Strait-of-Hormuz-if-its-benefits-denied-IRGC-Navy.

after a warning to withdraw them. That would put Trump under irresistible political pressure to order a retaliatory attack on Iranian military targets, such as radar and/or anti-aircraft installations.

As senior military officers have long been aware, however, U.S. military strategy for the Strait is not geared to gradual tit-for-tat escalation but to a quick effort to destroy Iran's means of retaliation. So the process is likely to quickly escalate out of control. Former commander of the Central Command in the Middle East, Gen. Charles Votel, told an interviewer that the idea of a retaliatory strike on Iran over the Saudi attack "presupposes a sequence that unfolds in an orderly, rational way"—which he called "a preposterous notion."[221]

In any crisis over an Iranian move to close the Strait of Hormuz, therefore, Trump would be subject to the combination of the accumulated domestic political pressures built up over many years of anti-Iran propaganda to hit back at Iran and a U.S. war plan geared to quick escalation to full-scale war.

The U.S. military knows that Iran has a critical geographical advantage in a battle over the Strait. As a U.S. Naval Intelligence analysis observed in 2017, the "vast miles of coastline" gives Iran "optimal firing positions for coastal defense cruise missiles", clearly implying that it would be difficult to target all of them.[222] And of course, it would be impossible to target the entire Iranian drone force, which the U.S. military now knows could reach not only U.S. ships and bases in the region but any target in the entire structure of U.S. military presence. Furthermore, Iran's military has a very strong incentive to unleash its retaliatory capabilities before the United States can maximize its destruction.

To avoid such a war Trump would have to abandon his whole program of "maximum pressure' and give up his bombastic approach to Iran in order to make a deal with Iran, based on a more realistic understanding of Iran's interests.

Trump's "Maximum Pressure" campaign, which is at the center of his Iran policy problem, was not merely an obstacle to U.S.-Iran diplomacy; it had actually been designed deliberately to lead to war. As one U.S. official— obviously unsympathetic to that initiative—told the *New York Times*, the

---

221. Quoted in Mark Bowden, "Top Military Officers Unload on Trump," *The Atlantic*, November 2019. https://www.theatlantic.com/magazine/archive/2019/11/military-officers-trump/598360/.
222. Iranian Naval Forces: A Tale of Two Navies (Washington, D.C.: Office of Naval intelligence, 2017), pp. 31-32. https://www.oni.navy.mil/Portals/12/Intel%20agencies/iran/Iran%20022217SP.pdf.

ultimate goal of the campaign for those who had designed it had always been to draw Iran into an armed conflict with the United States.[223]

The origins of the campaign bear out that official's observation. The lobbyist who had pushed for its adoption by the administration was Mark Dubowitz, the CEO of Foundation for the Defense of Democracies (FDD). FDD had been organized originally to "enhance Israel's image and the public's understanding of the issues affecting Israeli-Arab relations", according to its legal filing. But its main concern has always been to advance the interests of Likudist government in Israel—especially with regard to Iran. After Benjamin Netanyahu became Prime Minister in 2009, FDD sought to influence U.S. policy toward Iran in line with the policy of Netanyahu's government.[224]

That meant pushing primarily for military confrontation and/or regime change in Iran and opposing aggressively any diplomatic agreement with Tehran. Since 2011, Dubowitz has published a series of commentaries with FDD Senior Fellow Reuel Marc Gerecht, who had previously aggressively advocated U.S. bombing of Iran for years, in which they argued that such a confrontation would be necessary in the end. For Dubowitz and Gerecht, sanctions against Iran were never the primary objective. They argued in 2011 that sanctions were "an unavoidable prelude to any more forceful action to stop Ayatollah Khamenei's nuclear ambitions."[225]

After the United States and Iran agreed on an initial "Joint Program of Action" in November 2013, Dubowitz helped two key Israeli supporters funded heavily by AIPAC, Sen. Robert Menendez and Sen. Mark Kirk, write a bill that was clearly aimed at killing the negotiations. It demanded the dismantling of all Iranian nuclear facilities and an end to Iranian aid to Hezbollah and other regional allies—poison pills that would ensure that Congress would oppose the ultimate agreement.[226] In November 2014, Dubowitz and Gerecht warned that sanctions would "fail without other

223. Helene Cooper and Edward Wong, "Skeptical U.S. allies Resent Trump's New Claims of Threats from Iran," *New York Times*, May 14, 2019.

224. John B. Judis, "The Little Think Tank That Could," *Slate*, August 18, 2015.

225. Reuel Marc Gerecht, "To Bomb, or Not to Bomb," *The Weekly Standard*, April 24, 2006; Reuel Marc Gerecht and Mark Dubowitz, "Don't Give Up on Sanctions," *New York Times*, November 11, 2011.

226. Ali Gharib, "Exclusive: Top Senate Democrats Break with White House and Circulate New Iran Sanctions Bill," *Foreign Policy*, December 18, 201; Judis, "The Little Think Tank That Could."

forms of coercion" and suggested that Obama had only two choices: "launch military strikes or accept Iran as a nuclear state".[227]

When the final nuclear agreement was reached with Iran, Dubowitz developed new legislation with the same deal-killing demands. And in December 2016, at a Capitol Hill meeting of opponents of Obama's nuclear deal, he again warned that sanctions were "not a silver bullet" and again called for provoking war with Iran, suggesting that if an Iran ship harassed a U.S. warship, the U.S. sinking an Iranian ship "would be a good start".[228]

After Trump refused to certify the JCPOA in October 2017, Dubowitz worked closely with then–National Security Adviser H. R. McMaster on formulating administration demands that he knew very well would make any agreement with Iran impossible, and which Pompeo then presented publicly in May 2018. After Bolton became National Security Adviser, Dubowitz succeeded in getting FDD "senior adviser" Richard Goldberg as the Director for Countering Iranian Weapons of Mass Destruction in January 2019. Goldberg's main function was to sell the White House on the policy of ending all Iran's oil exports through extraterritorial sanctions. The Trump administration's decision to cut off all imports of Iranian oil by the remaining importing countries followed three months later.[229]

Dubowitz has made little, if any, effort to hide his real agenda on Iran policy. FDD and the financial and political figures behind it have maneuvered with great skill and determination through two administrations to provoke the Iran war crisis in which Trump now finds himself trapped. And they did so on behalf of the interests of Israel's Likudists, led for more than two decades by Benjamin Netanyahu.

The degree of influence acquired by the pro-Likud lobby over Trump administration Iran policy represented an unprecedented ability of a foreign country to determine whether the United States goes to war or not. But it is also a measure of the degree to which public understanding of the history of U.S.-Iran relations has so been grotesquely distorted that the pro-Israeli interests who have taken advantage of that fact can argue that the warlike policies they have pushed as being in the American interest. So, the issue of the overweening pro-Israel influence on the policy cannot be effectively

---

227. Reuel Marc Gerecht and Mark Dubowitz, "Iran's Diplomatic Path to a Bomb," *Wall Street Journal*, November 12, 2014.

228. Judis, "The Little Think Thank That Could"; Will Pearson, "Nuclear Deal Opponents Urge Military Confrontation with Iran," National Iranian-American Council (NIAC), December 18, 2016.

229. Humeyra Pamuk and Timothy Gardner, "How Trump's hawkish advisors won debate on Iran oil sanctions," *Reuters*, May 1, 2019.

address politically in the absence of a systematic process of relearning of that history.

Despite having been hemmed in by his advisers on Iran, Trump would like to find a way out of the crisis. Even as late as the UN General Assembly meeting in September 2019, Trump indicated his interest in negotiations with Iran, and offered a formula for suspending sanctions, but Rouhani refused. The impeachment process and the 2020 election, however, hold the keys to the unfolding of the Iran drama. On one hand impeachment made it less likely that—assuming Trump were to survive an impeachment vote in the Senate—he would be willing to go further toward Iran during an election year, given his base's attachment to the demonization of the Tehran regime.

On the other hand, Iran's strategy for counter-pressure on the United States during an election year certainly depends primarily on whether Trump would appear to sufficiently weakened relative to his 2016 electoral strength to hope for a Democratic victory. If Trump wins reelection, Iran would almost certainly resume the process of signaling to the United States that began in 2019. Without a sharp turn away from past U.S. policy, the process of escalating counter-moves and the risk of a slide into war would rise steeply. And the measure of the tragedy would be that it was predictable, but that the United States did not have the means to do what was necessary to avoid it.

Appendices: Documents on U.S. Iran Policy

Document No. 1: National Intelligence Estimate, "Iran: Nuclear Intentions and Capabilities," November 2007

source: https://www.dni.gov/files/documents/Newsroom/Reports%20and% 20Pubs/20071203_release.pdf.

(The National Intelligence Council produced an Intelligence Community (NIC)-coordinated National Intelligence Estimate in 2007 which concluded that in 2003 Iran halted a nuclear weapons program. That judgment was attacked by Bush administration figures and neoconservatives, because it made it more difficult for the administration to threaten Iran with an attack on its nuclear sites. But it also reaffirmed previous NIE's alleging that Iran had an active nuclear weapons program from 2000 to 2003 based on the assumption that intelligence documents purporting to show such a secret nuclear weapons program that suddenly surfaced in 2004 were authentic, despite clear evidence to the contrary [See Chapter 3]. Only the unclassified "Key Judgements" of the report were released to the public.)

Unclassified Key Judgments

Scope Note

This National Intelligence Estimate (NIE) assesses the status of Iran's nuclear program, and the program's outlook over the next 10 years. This time frame is more appropriate for estimating capabilities than intentions and foreign reactions, which are more difficult to estimate over a decade. In presenting the Intelligence Community's assessment of Iranian nuclear intentions and capabilities, the NIE thoroughly reviews all available information on these questions, examines the range of reasonable scenarios consistent with this information, and describes the key factors we judge would drive or impede nuclear progress in Iran. This NIE is an extensive reexamination of the issues in the May 2005 assessment.

This Estimate focuses on the following key questions:

- What are Iran's intentions toward developing nuclear weapons?
- What domestic factors affect Iran's decision-making on whether to develop nuclear weapons?
- What external factors affect Iran's decision-making on whether to develop nuclear weapons?
- What is the range of potential Iranian actions concerning the development of nuclear weapons, and the decisive factors that would lead Iran to choose one course of action over another?
- What is Iran's current and projected capability to develop nuclear weapons? What are our key assumptions, and Iran's key chokepoints/vulnerabilities?

This NIE does *not* assume that Iran intends to acquire nuclear weapons. Rather, it examines the intelligence to assess Iran's capability and intent (or lack thereof) to acquire nuclear weapons, taking full account of Iran's dual-use uranium fuel cycle and those nuclear activities that are at least partly civil in nature.

This Estimate does assume that the strategic goals and basic structure of Iran's senior leadership and government will remain similar to those that have endured since the death of Ayatollah Khomeini in 1989. We acknowledge the potential for these to change during the time frame of the Estimate, but are unable to confidently predict such changes or their implications. This Estimate does not assess how Iran may conduct future negotiations with the West on the nuclear issue.

This Estimate incorporates intelligence reporting available as of 31 October 2007.

Mean When We Say: An Explanation of Estimative Language

We use phrases such as *we judge, we assess,* and *we estimate*—and probabilistic terms such as *probably* and *likely*—to convey analytical assessments and judgments. Such statements are not facts, proof, or knowledge. These assessments and judgments generally are based on collected information, which often is incomplete or fragmentary. Some assessments are built on previous judgments. In all cases, assessments and judgments are not intended to imply that we have "proof" that shows something to be a fact or that definitively links two items or issues.

In addition to conveying judgments rather than certainty, our estimative language also often conveys 1) our assessed likelihood or probability of an event; and 2) the level of confidence we ascribe to the judgment.

Estimates of Likelihood. Because analytical judgments are not certain, we use probabilistic language to reflect the Community's estimates of the likelihood of developments or events. Terms such as *probably, likely, very likely,* or *almost certainly* indicate a greater than even chance. The terms *unlikely* and *remote* indicate a less than even chance that an event will occur; they do not imply that an event will not occur. Terms such as *might* or *may* reflect situations in which we are unable to assess the likelihood, generally because relevant information is unavailable, sketchy, or fragmented. Terms such as *we cannot dismiss, we cannot rule out,* or *we cannot discount* reflect an unlikely, improbable, or remote event whose consequences are such that it warrants mentioning. The chart provides a rough idea of the relationship of some of these terms to each other.

Remote/ Very Unlikely/ Unlikely/ Even Chance/ Probably or Likely / Very Likely / Almost Certainty

Confidence in Assessments. Our assessments and estimates are supported by information that varies in scope, quality and sourcing. Consequently, we ascribe *high, moderate,* or *low* levels of confidence to our assessments, as follows:

- *High confidence* generally indicates that our judgments are based on high-quality information, and/or that the nature of the issue makes it possible to render a solid judgment. A "high confidence" judgment is not a fact or a certainty, however, and such judgments still carry a risk of being wrong.

- *Moderate confidence* generally means that the information is credibly sourced and plausible but not of sufficient quality or corroborated sufficiently to warrant a higher level of confidence.
- *Low confidence* generally means that the information's credibility and/or plausibility is questionable, or that the information is too fragmented or poorly corroborated to make solid analytic inferences, or that we have significant concerns or problems with the sources.

Key Judgments

A. We judge with high confidence that in fall 2003, Tehran halted its nuclear weapons program[230]; we also assess with moderate-to-high confidence that Tehran at a minimum is keeping open the option to develop nuclear weapons. We judge with high confidence that the halt, and Tehran's announcement of its decision to suspend its declared uranium enrichment program and sign an Additional Protocol to its Nuclear Non-Proliferation Treaty Safeguards Agreement, was directed primarily in response to increasing international scrutiny and pressure resulting from exposure of Iran's previously undeclared nuclear work.

- We assess with high confidence that until fall 2003, Iranian military entities were working under government direction to develop nuclear weapons.
- We judge with high confidence that the halt lasted at least several years. (Because of intelligence gaps discussed elsewhere in this Estimate, however, DOE and the NIC assess with only moderate confidence that the halt to those activities represents a halt to Iran's entire nuclear weapons program.)
- We assess with moderate confidence Tehran had not restarted its nuclear weapons program as of mid-2007, but we do not know whether it currently intends to develop nuclear weapons.
- We continue to assess with moderate-to-high confidence that Iran does not currently have a nuclear weapon.

---

230. For the purposes of this Estimate, by "nuclear weapons program" we mean Iran's nuclear weapon design and weaponization work and covert uranium conversion-related and uranium enrichment-related work; we do not mean Iran's declared civil work related to uranium conversion and enrichment.

- Tehran's decision to halt its nuclear weapons program suggests it is less determined to develop nuclear weapons than we have been judging since 2005. Our assessment that the program probably was halted primarily in response to international pressure suggests Iran may be more vulnerable to influence on the issue than we judged previously.

B. We continue to assess with low confidence that Iran probably has imported at least some weapons-usable fissile material, but still judge with moderate-to-high confidence it has not obtained enough for a nuclear weapon. We cannot rule out that Iran has acquired from abroad—or will acquire in the future—a nuclear weapon or enough fissile material for a weapon. Barring such acquisitions, if Iran wants to have nuclear weapons it would need to produce sufficient amounts of fissile material indigenously—which we judge with high confidence it has not yet done.

C. We assess centrifuge enrichment is how Iran probably could first produce enough fissile material for a weapon, if it decides to do so. Iran resumed its declared centrifuge enrichment activities in January 2006, despite the continued halt in the nuclear weapons program. Iran made significant progress in 2007 installing centrifuges at Natanz, but we judge with moderate confidence it still faces significant technical problems operating them.

- We judge with moderate confidence that the earliest possible date Iran would be technically capable of producing enough HEU for a weapon is late 2009, but that this is very unlikely.
- We judge with moderate confidence Iran probably would be technically capable of producing enough HEU for a weapon sometime during the 2010-2015 time frame. (INR judges Iran is unlikely to achieve this capability before 2013 because of foreseeable technical and programmatic problems.) All agencies recognize the possibility that this capability may not be attained until *after* 2015.

D. Iranian entities are continuing to develop a range of technical capabilities that could be applied to producing nuclear weapons, if a decision is made to do so. For example, Iran's civilian uranium enrichment program is continuing. We also assess with high confidence that since fall 2003, Iran has been conducting research and development projects with commercial and conventional military applications—some of which would also be of limited use for nuclear weapons.

E. We do not have sufficient intelligence to judge confidently whether Tehran is willing to maintain the halt of its nuclear weapons program indefinitely while it weighs its options, or whether it will or already has set specific deadlines or criteria that will prompt it to restart the program.

- Our assessment that Iran halted the program in 2003 primarily in response to international pressure indicates Tehran's decisions are guided by a cost-benefit approach rather than a rush to a weapon irrespective of the political, economic, and military costs. This, in turn, suggests that some combination of threats of intensified international scrutiny and pressures, along with opportunities for Iran to achieve its security, prestige, and goals for regional influence in other ways, might—if perceived by Iran's leaders as credible—prompt Tehran to extend the current halt to its nuclear weapons program. It is difficult to specify what such a combination might be.
- We assess with moderate confidence that convincing the Iranian leadership to forgo the eventual development of nuclear weapons will be difficult given the linkage many within the leadership probably see between nuclear weapons development and Iran's key national security and foreign policy objectives, and given Iran's considerable effort from at least the late 1980s to 2003 to develop such weapons. In our judgment, only an Iranian political decision to abandon a nuclear weapons objective would plausibly keep Iran from eventually producing nuclear weapons—and such a decision is inherently reversible.

F. We assess with moderate confidence that Iran probably would use covert facilities—rather than its declared nuclear sites—for the production of highly enriched uranium for a weapon. A growing amount of intelligence indicates Iran was engaged in covert uranium conversion and uranium enrichment activity, but we judge that these efforts probably were halted in response to the fall 2003 halt, and that these efforts probably had not been restarted through at least mid-2007.

G. We judge with high confidence that Iran will not be technically capable of producing and reprocessing enough plutonium for a weapon before about 2015.

H. We assess with high confidence that Iran has the scientific, technical and industrial capacity eventually to produce nuclear weapons if it decides to do so.

Key Differences Between the Key Judgments of This Estimate on Iran's Nuclear Program and the May 2005 Assessment

2005 IC Estimate	2007 National Intelligence Estimate
Assess with high confidence that Iran currently is determined to develop nuclear weapons despite its international obligations and international pressure, but we do not assess that Iran is immovable.	Judge with high confidence that in fall 2003, Tehran halted its nuclear weapons program. Judge with high confidence that the halt lasted at least several years. (DOE and the NIC have moderate confidence that the halt to those activities represents a halt to Iran's entire nuclear weapons program.) Assess with moderate confidence Tehran had not restarted its nuclear weapons program as of mid-2007, but we do not know whether it currently intends to develop nuclear weapons. Judge with high confidence that the halt was directed primarily in response to increasing international scrutiny and pressure resulting from exposure of Iran's previously undeclared nuclear work. Assess with moderate-to-high confidence that Tehran at a minimum is keeping open the option to develop nuclear weapons.
We have moderate confidence in projecting when Iran is likely to make a nuclear weapon; we assess that it is unlikely before early-to-mid next decade.	We judge with moderate confidence that the earliest possible date Iran would be technically capable of producing enough highly enriched uranium (HEU) for a weapon is late 2009, but that this is very unlikely. We judge with moderate confidence Iran probably would be technically capable of producing enough HEU for a weapon sometime during the 2010-2015 time frame. (INR judges that Iran is unlikely to achieve this capability before 2013 because of foreseeable technical and programmatic problems.)
Iran could produce enough fissile material for a weapon by the end of this decade if it were to make more rapid and successful progress than we have seen to date.	We judge with moderate confidence that the earliest possible date Iran would be technically capable of producing enough highly enriched uranium (HEU) for a weapon is late 2009, but that this is very unlikely.

Document No. 2: United Nations Security Council Resolution 1803, March 3, 2008 [Extract]

source: https://www.iaea.org/sites/default/files/unsc_resolution2231-2015.pdf

(Under pressure from the U.S. government, the UN Security Council tried to put pressure on Iran to give up both its enrichment program and its ballistic missiles program. In articles 3, 9 and 10 it called on states and companies engaging in bilateral assistance, trade or financial transactions with Iranian companies "exercise vigilance" lest such transactions contribute to its nuclear or missile programs. The text cleverly suggesting that an Iranian company or bank doing business with Iran might be indirectly providing support to nuclear or missile programs through association with an Iranian entity that could be designated for its association with an alarming designated entity in the future. This language was an obvious ploy by the United States to intimidate foreign businesses by inducing a fear of future U.S. economic sanctions against them.)

3. Calls upon all States to exercise vigilance and restraint regarding the entry into or transit through their territories of individuals who are engaged in, directly associated with or providing support for Iran's proliferation sensitive nuclear activities or for the development of nuclear weapon delivery systems, and decides in this regard that all States shall notify the Committee established pursuant to paragraph 18 of resolution 1737 (2006) (herein "the Committee") of the entry into or transit through their territories of the persons designated in the Annex to resolution 1737 (2006), Annex I to resolution 1747 (2007) or Annex I to this resolution, as well as of additional persons designated by the Security Council or the Committee as being engaged in, directly associated with or providing support for Iran's proliferation sensitive nuclear activities or for the development of nuclear weapon delivery systems, including through the involvement in procurement of the prohibited items, goods, equipment, materials and technology specified by and under the measures in paragraphs 3 and 4 of resolution 1737 (2006), except where such entry or transit is for activities directly related to the items in subparagraphs 3 (b) (i) and (ii) of resolution 1737 (2006);

4. Underlines that nothing in paragraph 3 above requires a State to refuse its own nationals entry into its territory, and that all States shall, in the implementation of the above paragraph, take into account humanitarian considerations, including religious obligations, as well as the necessity to meet the

objectives of this resolution, resolution 1737 (2006) and resolution 1747 (2007), including where Article XV of the IAEA Statute is engaged;

5. Decides that all States shall take the necessary measures to prevent the entry into or transit through their territories of individuals designated in Annex II to this resolution as well as of additional persons designated by the Security Council or the Committee as being engaged in, directly associated with or providing support for Iran's proliferation sensitive nuclear activities or for the development of nuclear weapon delivery systems, including through the involvement in procurement of the prohibited items, goods, equipment, materials and technology specified by and under the measures in paragraphs 3 and 4 of resolution 1737 (2006), except where such entry or transit is for activities directly related to the items in subparagraphs 3 (b) (i) and (ii) of resolution 1737 (2006) and provided that nothing in this paragraph shall oblige a State to refuse its own nationals entry into its territory;

6. Decides that the measures imposed by paragraph 5 above shall not apply where the Committee determines on a case-by-case basis that such travel is justified on the grounds of humanitarian need, including religious obligations, or where the Committee concludes that an exemption would otherwise further the objectives of the present resolution;

7. Decides that the measures specified in paragraphs 12, 13, 14 and 15 of resolution 1737 (2006) shall apply also to the persons and entities listed in Annexes I and III to this resolution, and any persons or entities acting on their behalf or at their direction, and to entities owned or controlled by them and to persons and entities determined by the Council or the Committee to have assisted designated persons or entities in evading sanctions of, or in violating the provisions of, this resolution, resolution 1737 (2006) or resolution 1747 (2007);

8. Decides that all States shall take the necessary measures to prevent the supply, sale or transfer directly or indirectly from their territories or by their nationals or using their flag vessels or aircraft to, or for use in or benefit of, Iran, and whether or not originating in their territories, of:

   a. all items, materials, equipment, goods and technology set out in INFCIRC/254/Rev.7/Part 2 of document S/2006/814, except the supply, sale or transfer, in accordance with the requirements of paragraph 5 of resolution 1737 (2006), of items, materials, equipment, goods and technology set out in sections 1 and 2 of the Annex to that document, and sections 3 to 6 as notified in advance to the Committee, only when for exclusive use in light water reactors, and where such supply, sale or transfer is necessary for technical cooperation provided to Iran

by the IAEA or under its auspices as provided for in paragraph 16 of
resolution 1737 (2006);

b. all items, materials, equipment, goods and technology set out in
19.A.3 of Category II of document S/2006/815;

9. Calls upon all States to exercise vigilance in entering into new commitments for public provided financial support for trade with Iran, including the
granting of export credits, guarantees or insurance, to their nationals or entities involved in such trade, in order to avoid such financial support contributing to the proliferation sensitive nuclear activities, or to the development
of nuclear weapon delivery systems, as referred to in resolution 1737 (2006);
10. Calls upon all States to exercise vigilance over the activities of financial
institutions in their territories with all banks domiciled in Iran, in particular with Bank Melli and Bank Saderat, and their branches and subsidiaries
abroad, in order to avoid such activities contributing to the proliferation
sensitive nuclear activities, or to the development of nuclear weapon delivery systems, as referred to in resolution 1737 (2006);
11. Calls upon all States, in accordance with their national legal authorities
and legislation and consistent with international law, in particular the law of
the sea and relevant international civil aviation agreements, to inspect the
cargoes to and from Iran, of aircraft and vessels, at their airports and seaports,
owned or operated by Iran Air Cargo and Islamic Republic of Iran Shipping
Line, provided there are reasonable grounds to believe that the aircraft or
vessel is transporting goods prohibited under this resolution or resolution
1737 (2006) or resolution 1747 (2007);
12. Requires all States, in cases when inspection mentioned in the paragraph
above is undertaken, to submit to the Security Council within five working
days a written report on the inspection containing, in particular, explanation of the grounds for the inspection, as well as information on its time,
place, circumstances, results and other relevant details;
13. Calls upon all States to report to the Committee within 60 days of the
adoption of this resolution on the steps they have taken with a view to
implementing effectively paragraphs 3, 5, 7, 8, 9, 10 and 11 above;
14. Decides that the mandate of the Committee as set out in paragraph 18
of resolution 1737 (2006) shall also apply to the measures imposed in resolution 1747 (2007) and this resolution;

Document No. 3: United Nations Security Council Resolution 1929, June 9, 2010 [Extract].

source: https://www.iaea.org/sites/default/files/unsc_res1929-2010.pdf

(Security Council Resolution 1929 went much further in an effort to intimidate businesses and banks contemplating business arrangement with Iranian entities, as discussed in Chapter 6. Its tricky language, written by the U.S. Treasury Department called on states to prevent banks from providing financial services to Iran, to inspect all cargo to and from Iran in their territory, and to prohibit banks from entering to new partnerships with Iranian banks or opening new offices in Iran, if it has "information that provides reasonable grounds to believe" that it would contribute to Iran nuclear or missile program. It was the template used in the Trump administration for "Maximum Pressure" at the behest of the Foundation for the Defense of Democracies)

18. Decides that all States shall prohibit the provision by their nationals or from their territory of bunkering services, such as provision of fuel or sup-plies, or other servicing of vessels, to Iranian-owned or -contracted vessels, including chartered vessels, if they have information that provides reason-able grounds to believe they are carrying items the supply, sale, transfer, or export of which is prohibited by paragraphs 3, 4 or 7 of resolution 1737 (2006), paragraph 5 of resolution 1747 (2007), paragraph 8 of resolution 1803 (2008) or paragraphs 8 or 9 of this resolution, unless provision of such services is necessary for humanitarian purposes or until such time as the cargo has been inspected, and seized and disposed of if necessary, and underlines that this paragraph is not intended to affect legal economic activities;

19. Decides that the measures specified in paragraphs 12, 13, 14 and 15 of resolution 1737 (2006) shall also apply to the entities of the Islamic Republic of Iran Shipping Lines (IRISL) as specified in Annex III and to any person or entity acting on their behalf or at their direction, and to entities owned or controlled by them, including through illicit means, or determined by the Council or the Committee to have assisted them in evading the sanctions of, or in violating the provisions of, resolutions 1737 (2006), 1747 (2007), 1803 (2008) or this resolution;

20. Requests all Member States to communicate to the Committee any information available on transfers or activity by Iran Air's cargo division or vessels owned or operated by the Islamic Republic of Iran Shipping Lines

(IRISL) to other companies that may have been undertaken in order to evade the sanctions of, or in violation of the provisions of, resolutions 1737 (2006), 1747 (2007), 1803 (2008) or this resolution, including renaming or re-registering of aircraft, vessels or ships, and requests the Committee to make that information widely available;

21. Calls upon all States, in addition to implementing their obligations pursuant to resolutions 1737 (2006), 1747 (2007), 1803 (2008) and this resolution, to prevent the provision of financial services, including insurance or re-insurance, or the transfer to, through, or from their territory, or to or by their nationals or entities organized under their laws (including branches abroad), or persons or financial institutions in their territory, of any financial or other assets or resources if they have information that provides reasonable grounds to believe that such services, assets or resources could contribute to Iran's proliferation-sensitive nuclear activities, or the development of nuclear weapon delivery systems, including by freezing any financial or other assets or resources on their territories or that hereafter come within their territories, or that are subject to their jurisdiction or that hereafter become subject to their jurisdiction, that are related to such programmes or activities and applying enhanced monitoring to prevent all such transactions in accordance with their national authorities and legislation;

22. Decides that all States shall require their nationals, persons subject to their jurisdiction and firms incorporated in their territory or subject to their jurisdiction to exercise vigilance when doing business with entities incorporated in Iran or subject to Iran's jurisdiction, including those of the IRGC and IRISL, and any individuals or entities acting on their behalf or at their direction, and entities owned or controlled by them, including through illicit means, if they have information that provides reasonable grounds to believe that such business could contribute to Iran's proliferation-sensitive nuclear activities or the development of nuclear weapon delivery systems or to violations of resolutions 1737 (2006), 1747 (2007), 1803 (2008) or this resolution;

23. Calls upon States to take appropriate measures that prohibit in their territories the opening of new branches, subsidiaries, or representative offices of Iranian banks, and also that prohibit Iranian banks from establishing new joint ventures, taking an ownership interest in or establishing or maintaining correspondent relationships with banks in their jurisdiction to prevent the provision of financial services if they have information that provides reasonable grounds to believe that these activities could contribute to Iran's proliferation-sensitive nuclear activities or the development of nuclear weapon delivery systems;

24. Calls upon States to take appropriate measures that prohibit financial institutions within their territories or under their jurisdiction from opening representative offices or subsidiaries or banking accounts in Iran if they have information that provides reasonable grounds to believe that such financial services could contribute to Iran's proliferation-sensitive nuclear activities or the development of nuclear weapon delivery systems;

Document No. 4: Remarks by President Trump on Iran Strategy, October 13, 2017

source: https://www.whitehouse.gov/briefings-statements/remarks-president-trump-iran-strategy/.

(In his first major policy statement on Iran Trump portrayed Iran as an demonic regime that poses a dire threat to the United States, attacked the Iran nuclear deal, vowed to counter Iranian "destabilization" in the region and support for "terrorist proxies", go after its missile program, add sanctions to block is financing of "terror" and prevent Iran from getting a nuclear weapon.)

THE PRESIDENT: Thank you very much. My fellow Americans: As President of the United States, my highest obligation is to ensure the safety and security of the American people.

History has shown that the longer we ignore a threat, the more dangerous that threat becomes. For this reason, upon taking office, I've ordered a complete strategic review of our policy toward the rogue regime in Iran. That review is now complete.

Today, I am announcing our strategy, along with several major steps we are taking to confront the Iranian regime's hostile actions and to ensure that Iran never, and I mean never, acquires a nuclear weapon.

Our policy is based on a clear-eyed assessment of the Iranian dictatorship, its sponsorship of terrorism, and its continuing aggression in the Middle East and all around the world.

Iran is under the control of a fanatical regime that seized power in 1979 and forced a proud people to submit to its extremist rule. This radical regime has raided the wealth of one of the world's oldest and most vibrant nations, and spread death, destruction, and chaos all around the globe.

Beginning in 1979, agents of the Iranian regime illegally seized the U.S. embassy in Tehran and held more than 60 Americans hostage during the 444 days of the crisis. The Iranian-backed terrorist group Hezbollah twice bombed our embassy in Lebanon—once in 1983 and again in 1984. Another Iranian-supported bombing killed 241 Americans—service members they were, in their barracks in Beirut in 1983.

In 1996, the regime directed another bombing of American military housing in Saudi Arabia, murdering 19 Americans in cold blood.

Iranian proxies provided training to operatives who were later involved in al Qaeda's bombing of the American embassies in Kenya, Tanzania, and two years later, killing 224 people, and wounding more than 4,000 others.

The regime harbored high-level terrorists in the wake of the 9/11 attacks, including Osama bin Laden's son. In Iraq and Afghanistan, groups supported by Iran have killed hundreds of American military personnel.

The Iranian dictatorship's aggression continues to this day. The regime remains the world's leading state sponsor of terrorism, and provides assistance to al Qaeda, the Taliban, Hezbollah, Hamas, and other terrorist networks. It develops, deploys, and proliferates missiles that threaten American troops and our allies. It harasses American ships and threatens freedom of navigation in the Arabian Gulf and in the Red Sea. It imprisons Americans on false charges. And it launches cyberattacks against our critical infrastructure, financial system, and military.

The United States is far from the only target of the Iranian dictatorship's long campaign of bloodshed. The regime violently suppresses its own citizens; it shot unarmed student protestors in the street during the Green Revolution.

This regime has fueled sectarian violence in Iraq, and vicious civil wars in Yemen and Syria. In Syria, the Iranian regime has supported the atrocities of Bashar al-Assad's regime and condoned Assad's use of chemical weapons against helpless civilians, including many, many children.

Given the regime's murderous past and present, we should not take lightly its sinister vision for the future. The regime's two favorite chants are "Death to America" and "Death to Israel."

Realizing the gravity of the situation, the United States and the United Nations Security Council sought, over many years, to stop Iran's pursuit of nuclear weapons with a wide array of strong economic sanctions.

But the previous administration lifted these sanctions, just before what would have been the total collapse of the Iranian regime, through the deeply controversial 2015 nuclear deal with Iran. This deal is known as the Joint Comprehensive Plan of Action, or JCPOA.

As I have said many times, the Iran Deal was one of the worst and most one-sided transactions the United States has ever entered into. The same mindset that produced this deal is responsible for years of terrible trade deals that have sacrificed so many millions of jobs in our country to the benefit of other countries. We need negotiators who will much more strongly represent America's interest.

The nuclear deal threw Iran's dictatorship a political and economic lifeline, providing urgently needed relief from the intense domestic pressure the sanctions had created. It also gave the regime an immediate financial boost and over $100 billion dollars its government could use to fund terrorism.

The regime also received a massive cash settlement of $1.7 billion from the United States, a large portion of which was physically loaded onto an airplane and flown into Iran. Just imagine the sight of those huge piles of money being hauled off by the Iranians waiting at the airport for the cash. I wonder where all that money went.

Worst of all, the deal allows Iran to continue developing certain elements of its nuclear program. And importantly, in just a few years, as key restrictions disappear, Iran can sprint towards a rapid nuclear weapons breakout. In other words, we got weak inspections in exchange for no more than a purely short-term and temporary delay in Iran's path to nuclear weapons.

What is the purpose of a deal that, at best, only delays Iran's nuclear capability for a short period of time? This, as President of the United States, is unacceptable. In other countries, they think in terms of 100-year intervals, not just a few years at a time.

The saddest part of the deal for the United States is that all of the money was paid up front, which is unheard of, rather than at the end of the deal when they have shown they've played by the rules. But what's done is done, and that's why we are where we are.

Iranian regime has committed multiple violations of the agreement. For example, on two separate occasions, they have exceeded the limit of 130 metric tons of heavy water. Until recently, the Iranian regime has also failed to meet our expectations in its operation of advanced centrifuges.

The Iranian regime has also intimidated international inspectors into not using the full inspection authorities that the agreement calls for.

Iranian officials and military leaders have repeatedly claimed they will not allow inspectors onto military sites, even though the international community suspects some of those sites were part of Iran's clandestine nuclear weapons program.

There are also many people who believe that Iran is dealing with North Korea. I am going to instruct our intelligence agencies to do a thorough analysis and report back their findings beyond what they have already reviewed.

By its own terms, the Iran Deal was supposed to contribute to "regional and international peace and security." And yet, while the United States adheres to our commitment under the deal, the Iranian regime continues to fuel conflict, terror, and turmoil throughout the Middle East and beyond. Importantly, Iran is not living up to the spirit of the deal.

So today, in recognition of the increasing menace posed by Iran, and after extensive consultations with our allies, I am announcing a new strategy to address the full range of Iran's destructive actions.

First, we will work with our allies to counter the regime's destabilizing activity and support for terrorist proxies in the region.

Second, we will place additional sanctions on the regime to block their financing of terror.

Third, we will address the regime's proliferation of missiles and weapons that threaten its neighbors, global trade, and freedom of navigation.

And finally, we will deny the regime all paths to a nuclear weapon.

Today, I am also announcing several major steps my administration is taking in pursuit of this strategy.

The execution of our strategy begins with the long-overdue step of imposing tough sanctions on Iran's Islamic Revolutionary Guard Corps. The Revolutionary Guard is the Iranian Supreme Leader's corrupt personal terror force and militia. It has hijacked large portions of Iran's economy and seized massive religious endowments to fund war and terror abroad. This includes arming the Syrian dictator, supplying proxies and partners with missiles and weapons to attack civilians in the region, and even plotting to bomb a popular restaurant right here in Washington, D.C.

I am authorizing the Treasury Department to further sanction the entire Islamic Revolutionary Guard Corps for its support for terrorism and to apply sanctions to its officials, agents, and affiliates. I urge our allies to join us in taking strong actions to curb Iran's continued dangerous and destabilizing behavior, including thorough sanctions outside the Iran Deal that target the regime's ballistic missile program, in support for terrorism, and all of its destructive activities, of which there are many.

Finally, on the grave matter of Iran's nuclear program: Since the signing of the nuclear agreement, the regime's dangerous aggression has only escalated. At the same time, it has received massive sanctions relief while continuing to develop its missiles program. Iran has also entered into lucrative business contracts with other parties to the agreement.

When the agreement was finalized in 2015, Congress passed the Iran Nuclear Agreement Review Act to ensure that Congress's voice would be heard on the deal. Among other conditions, this law requires the President, or his designee, to certify that the suspension of sanctions under the deal is "appropriate and proportionate" to measure—and other measures taken by Iran to terminate its illicit nuclear program. Based on the factual record I have put forward, I am announcing today that we cannot and will not make this certification.

We will not continue down a path whose predictable conclusion is more violence, more terror, and the very real threat of Iran's nuclear breakout.

That is why I am directing my administration to work closely with Congress and our allies to address the deal's many serious flaws so that the Iranian regime can never threaten the world with nuclear weapons. These include the deal's sunset clauses that, in just a few years, will eliminate key restrictions on Iran's nuclear program.

The flaws in the deal also include insufficient enforcement and near total silence on Iran's missile programs. Congress has already begun the work to address these problems. Key House and Senate leaders are drafting legislation that would amend the Iran Nuclear Agreement Review Act to strengthen enforcement, prevent Iran from developing an inter-—this is so totally important—an intercontinental ballistic missile, and make all restrictions on Iran's nuclear activity permanent under U.S. law. So important. I support these initiatives.

However, in the event we are not able to reach a solution working with Congress and our allies, then the agreement will be terminated. It is under continuous review, and our participation can be cancelled by me, as President, at any time.

As we have seen in North Korea, the longer we ignore a threat, the worse that threat becomes. It is why we are determined that the world's leading sponsor of terrorism will never obtain nuclear weapons.

In this effort, we stand in total solidarity with the Iranian regime's longest-suffering victims: its own people. The citizens of Iran have paid a heavy price for the violence and extremism of their leaders. The Iranian people long to—and they just are longing, to reclaim their country's proud history, its culture, its civilization, its cooperation with its neighbors.

We hope that these new measures directed at the Iranian dictatorship will compel the government to reevaluate its pursuit of terror at the expense of its people.

We hope that our actions today will help bring about a future of peace, stability, and prosperity in the Middle East — a future where sovereign nations respect each other and their own citizens.

We pray for a future where young children—American and Iranian, Muslim, Christian, and Jewish—can grow up in a world free from violence, hatred, and terror.

And, until that blessed day comes, we will do what we must to keep America safe.

Thank you, God bless you, and God bless America. Thank you.

Document No. 5: Statement by the President on the Iran Nuclear Deal, January 12, 2018

source: https://www.whitehouse.gov/briefings-statements/statement-president-iran-nuclear-deal/

(President Trump declared that he would withdraw from the Iran nuclear deal unless and reimposed sanctions announced unless Iran agreed to meet four major demands for changes in the 2015 agreement, which Iran had carried out to the satisfaction of the International Atomic Energy Agency. The four conditions included making all of the limitations on its nuclear program in the agreement permanent and giving up its ballistic missile program.)

The Iranian regime is the world's leading state sponsor of terror. It enables Hezbollah, Hamas, and many other terrorists to sow chaos and kill innocent people. It has funded, armed, and trained more than 100,000 militants to spread destruction across the Middle East. It props up the murderous regime of Bashar al Assad, and has helped him slaughter his own people. The regime's destructive missiles threaten neighboring countries and international shipping. Within Iran, the Supreme Leader and his Islamic Revolutionary Guard Corps use mass arrests and torture to oppress and silence Iran's people. Iran's ruling elite has let their citizens go hungry while enriching themselves by stealing Iran's national wealth

Last October, I outlined to the American people—and to the world—my strategy for confronting these and other destructive activities. We are countering Iranian proxy wars in Yemen and Syria. We are cutting off the regime's money flows to terrorists. We have sanctioned nearly 100 individuals and entities involved with the Iranian regime's ballistic missile program and its other illicit activities. Today, I am adding 14 more to the sanctions list. We are also supporting the brave Iranian citizens who are demanding change from a corrupt regime that wastes the Iranian people's money on weapons systems at home and terrorism abroad. And crucially, we are calling on all nations to lend similar support to the Iranian people, who are suffering under a regime that is stifling basic freedoms and denying its citizens the opportunity to build better lives for their families—an opportunity that is every human being's God-given right.

All this stands in stark contrast to the policy and actions of the previous administration. President Obama failed to act as the Iranian people took to the streets in 2009. He turned a blind eye as Iran built and tested dangerous missiles and exported terror. He curried favor with the Iranian regime in order to push through the disastrously flawed Iran nuclear deal.

I have been very clear about my opinion of that deal. It gave Iran far too much in exchange for far too little. The enormous financial windfall the Iranian regime received because of the deal—access to more than $100 billion, including $1.8 billion in cash—has not been used to better the lives of the Iranian people. Instead, it has served as a slush fund for weapons, terror, and oppression, and to further line the pockets of corrupt regime leaders. The Iranian people know this, which is one reason why so many have taken to the streets to express their outrage.

Despite my strong inclination, I have not yet withdrawn the United States from the Iran nuclear deal. Instead, I have outlined two possible paths forward: either fix the deal's disastrous flaws, or the United States will withdraw.

I am open to working with Congress on bipartisan legislation regarding Iran. But any bill I sign must include four critical components.

First, it must demand that Iran allow immediate inspections at all sites requested by international inspectors.

Second, it must ensure that Iran never even comes close to possessing a nuclear weapon.

Third, unlike the nuclear deal, these provisions must have no expiration date. My policy is to deny Iran all paths to a nuclear weapon—not just for ten years, but forever.

If Iran does not comply with any of these provisions, American nuclear sanctions would automatically resume.

Fourth, the legislation must explicitly state in United States law—for the first time—that long-range missile and nuclear weapons programs are inseparable, and that Iran's development and testing of missiles should be subject to severe sanctions.

In 2015, the Obama Administration foolishly traded away strong multilateral sanctions to get its weak nuclear deal. By contrast, my Administration has engaged with key European allies in seeking to secure a new supplemental agreement that would impose new multilateral sanctions if Iran develops or tests long-range missiles, thwarts inspections, or makes progress toward a nuclear weapon—requirements that should have been in the nuclear deal in the first place. And, like the bill I expect from Congress, these provisions of a supplemental agreement must never expire.

I also call on all our allies to take stronger steps with us to confront Iran's other malign activities. Among other actions, our allies should cut off funding to the Islamic Revolutionary Guard Corps, its militant proxies, and anyone else who contributes to Iran's support for terrorism. They should designate Hezbollah—in its entirety—as a terrorist organization. They should join us in constraining Iran's missile development and stopping its proliferation of missiles, especially to Yemen. They should join us in countering Iran's cyber threats. They should help us deter Iran's aggression against international shipping. They should pressure the Iranian regime to stop violating its citizens' rights. And they should not do business with groups that enrich Iran's dictatorship or fund the Revolutionary Guard and its terrorist proxies.

Today, I am waiving the application of certain nuclear sanctions, but only in order to secure our European allies' agreement to fix the terrible flaws of the Iran nuclear deal. This is a last chance. In the absence of such an agreement, the United States will not again waive sanctions in order to stay in the Iran nuclear deal. And if at any time I judge that such an agreement is not within reach, I will withdraw from the deal immediately.

No one should doubt my word. I said I would not certify the nuclear deal—and I did not. I will also follow through on this pledge. I hereby call on key European countries to join with the United States in fixing significant flaws in the deal, countering Iranian aggression, and supporting the Iranian people. If other nations fail to act during this time, I will terminate our deal with Iran. Those who, for whatever reason, choose not to work with us will be siding with the Iranian regime's nuclear ambitions, and against the people of Iran and the peaceful nations of the world.

Document No. 6: Remarks by President Trump on the Joint Comprehensive Plan of Action, May 8, 2018

source: https://www.whitehouse.gov/briefings-statements/remarks-president-trump-joint-comprehensive-plan-action/

(On May 8, 2018, President Trump formally announced the U.S. withdrawal from the Joint Comprehensive Plan of Action and signed a proclamation reinstating the nuclear-related sanctions that had been removed under that agreement, thus establishing the legal basis for his administration's "Maximum Pressure" campaign aimed at preventing Iran from being able export oil—and making an eventual war with Iran a serious possibility.)

THE PRESIDENT: My fellow Americans: Today, I want to update the world on our efforts to prevent Iran from acquiring a nuclear weapon.

The Iranian regime is the leading state sponsor of terror. It exports dangerous missiles, fuels conflicts across the Middle East, and supports terrorist proxies and militias such as Hezbollah, Hamas, the Taliban, and al Qaeda.

Over the years, Iran and its proxies have bombed American embassies and military installations, murdered hundreds of American servicemembers, and kidnapped, imprisoned, and tortured American citizens. The Iranian regime has funded its long reign of chaos and terror by plundering the wealth of its own people.

No action taken by the regime has been more dangerous than its pursuit of nuclear weapons and the means of delivering them.

In 2015, the previous administration joined with other nations in a deal regarding Iran's nuclear program. This agreement was known as the Joint Comprehensive Plan of Action, or JCPOA.

In theory, the so-called "Iran deal" was supposed to protect the United States and our allies from the lunacy of an Iranian nuclear bomb, a weapon that will only endanger the survival of the Iranian regime. In fact, the deal allowed Iran to continue enriching uranium and, over time, reach the brink of a nuclear breakout.

The deal lifted crippling economic sanctions on Iran in exchange for very weak limits on the regime's nuclear activity, and no limits at all on its other malign behavior, including its sinister activities in Syria, Yemen, and other places all around the world.

In other words, at the point when the United States had maximum leverage, this disastrous deal gave this regime—and it's a regime of great terror—many billions of dollars, some of it in actual cash—a great embarrassment to me as a citizen and to all citizens of the United States.

A constructive deal could easily have been struck at the time, but it wasn't. At the heart of the Iran deal was a giant fiction that a murderous regime desired only a peaceful nuclear energy program.

Today, we have definitive proof that this Iranian promise was a lie. Last week, Israel published intelligence documents long concealed by Iran, conclusively showing the Iranian regime and its history of pursuing nuclear weapons.

The fact is this was a horrible, one-sided deal that should have never, ever been made. It didn't bring calm, it didn't bring peace, and it never will.

In the years since the deal was reached, Iran's military budget has grown by almost 40 percent, while its economy is doing very badly. After the sanctions were lifted, the dictatorship used its new funds to build nuclear-capable missiles, support terrorism, and cause havoc throughout the Middle East and beyond.

The agreement was so poorly negotiated that even if Iran fully complies, the regime can still be on the verge of a nuclear breakout in just a short period of time. The deal's sunset provisions are totally unacceptable. If I allowed this deal to stand, there would soon be a nuclear arms race in the Middle East. Everyone would want their weapons ready by the time Iran had theirs.

Making matters worse, the deal's inspection provisions lack adequate mechanisms to prevent, detect, and punish cheating, and don't even have the unqualified right to inspect many important locations, including military facilities.

Not only does the deal fail to halt Iran's nuclear ambitions, but it also fails to address the regime's development of ballistic missiles that could deliver nuclear warheads.

Finally, the deal does nothing to constrain Iran's destabilizing activities, including its support for terrorism. Since the agreement, Iran's bloody ambitions have grown only more brazen.

In light of these glaring flaws, I announced last October that the Iran deal must either be renegotiated or terminated.

Three months later, on January 12th, I repeated these conditions. I made clear that if the deal could not be fixed, the United States would no longer be a party to the agreement.

Over the past few months, we have engaged extensively with our allies and partners around the world, including France, Germany, and the United Kingdom. We have also consulted with our friends from across the Middle

East. We are unified in our understanding of the threat and in our conviction that Iran must never acquire a nuclear weapon.

After these consultations, it is clear to me that we cannot prevent an Iranian nuclear bomb under the decaying and rotten structure of the current agreement.

The Iran deal is defective at its core. If we do nothing, we know exactly what will happen. In just a short period of time, the world's leading state sponsor of terror will be on the cusp of acquiring the world's most dangerous weapons.

Therefore, I am announcing today that the United States will withdraw from the Iran nuclear deal.

In a few moments, I will sign a presidential memorandum to begin reinstating U.S. nuclear sanctions on the Iranian regime. We will be instituting the highest level of economic sanction. Any nation that helps Iran in its quest for nuclear weapons could also be strongly sanctioned by the United States.

America will not be held hostage to nuclear blackmail. We will not allow American cities to be threatened with destruction. And we will not allow a regime that chants "Death to America" to gain access to the most deadly weapons on Earth.

Today's action sends a critical message: The United States no longer makes empty threats. When I make promises, I keep them. In fact, at this very moment, Secretary Pompeo is on his way to North Korea in preparation for my upcoming meeting with Kim Jong-un. Plans are being made. Relationships are building. Hopefully, a deal will happen and, with the help of China, South Korea, and Japan, a future of great prosperity and security can be achieved for everyone.

As we exit the Iran deal, we will be working with our allies to find a real, comprehensive, and lasting solution to the Iranian nuclear threat. This will include efforts to eliminate the threat of Iran's ballistic missile program; to stop its terrorist activities worldwide; and to block its menacing activity across the Middle East. In the meantime, powerful sanctions will go into full effect. If the regime continues its nuclear aspirations, it will have bigger problems than it has ever had before.

Finally, I want to deliver a message to the long-suffering people of Iran: The people of America stand with you. It has now been almost 40 years since this dictatorship seized power and took a proud nation hostage. Most of Iran's 80 million citizens have sadly never known an Iran that prospered in peace with its neighbors and commanded the admiration of the world.

But the future of Iran belongs to its people. They are the rightful heirs to a rich culture and an ancient land. And they deserve a nation that does justice to their dreams, honor to their history, and glory to God.

Iran's leaders will naturally say that they refuse to negotiate a new deal; they refuse. And that's fine. I'd probably say the same thing if I was in their position. But the fact is they are going to want to make a new and lasting deal, one that benefits all of Iran and the Iranian people. When they do, I am ready, willing, and able.

Great things can happen for Iran, and great things can happen for the peace and stability that we all want in the Middle East.

There has been enough suffering, death, and destruction. Let it end now.

Thank you. God bless you. Thank you.

(The presidential memorandum is signed.)

Document No. 7: Speech by Secretary of State Mike Pompeo, May 21, 2018

source: https://mfa.gov.il/MFA/ForeignPolicy/Iran/Pages/US-Sec--State-Pompeo-a-new-Iran-strategy-21-May-2018.aspx.

(Secretary of State Mike Pompeo's speech at The Heritage Foundation in May 2018 outlined a new, more militant Trump Administration's policy toward Iran that made twelve demands as conditions for removing the sanctions aimed at bringing the Iranian economy it its knees. that were widely recognized as closing the door to negotiations with Iran in practice.)

SECRETARY POMPEO: Well, good morning, everyone. I first want to thank the Heritage Foundation and its president, Kay Coles James. Thank you for hosting me today. First as a private citizen and then as a member of Congress, and even today, the Heritage Foundation has shaped my thinking on matters of the world and public policy issues. I'm grateful for that excellent work.

And thanks for reminding me I can't talk about anything else but what we're talking about today. (Laughter.) Three years on. But it's an honor to be here.

Two weeks ago, President Trump terminated the United States participation in the Joint Comprehensive Plan of Action, more commonly known as the Iran nuclear deal.

President Trump withdrew from the deal for a simple reason: it failed to guarantee the safety of the American people from the risk created by the leaders of the Islamic Republic of Iran.

No more. No more wealth creation for Iranian kleptocrats. No more acceptance of missiles landing in Riyadh and in the Golan Heights. No more cost-free expansions of Iranian power. No more.

The JCPOA put the world at risk because of its fatal flaws.

And they're worth recounting at some length today, if only for the purpose of ensuring that subsequent arrangements do not repeat them.

For example, the weak sunset provisions of the JCPOA merely delayed the inevitable nuclear weapons capability of the Iranian regime.

After the countdown clock ran out on the deal's sunset provisions, Iran would be free for a quick sprint to the bomb, setting off a potentially catastrophic arms race in the region. Indeed, the very brevity of the delay in the Iranian nuclear program itself incentivized Middle Eastern proliferation.

Moreover, as we have seen from Israel's recent remarkable intelligence operation, Iran has lied for years about having had a nuclear weapons program. Iran entered into the JCPOA in bad faith. It is worth noting that even today, the regime continues to lie.

Just last month, Iranian Foreign Minister Zarif told a Sunday morning news show, "We never wanted to produce a bomb."

This claim—this claim would be laughable if not for the willful deception behind it. Not only did the AMAD Program exist; the Iranians took great care—though, as we can see now, not enough care—to protect, hide, and preserve the work of Mohsen Fakhrizadeh Mahabadi and his gang of nuclear scientists.

The JCPOA had additional shortcomings as well.

The mechanisms for inspecting and verifying Iran's compliance with the deal were simply not strong enough.

The deal did nothing to address Iran's continuing development of ballistic and cruise missiles, which could deliver nuclear warheads.

The JCPOA permitted the Iranian regime to use the money from the JCPOA to boost the economic fortunes of a struggling people, but the regime's leaders refused to do so.

Instead, the government spent its newfound treasure fueling proxy wars across the Middle East and lining the pockets of the Islamic Revolutionary Guard Corps, Hizballah, Hamas, and the Houthis.

Remember: Iran advanced its march across the Middle East during the JCPOA. Qasem Soleimani has been playing with house money that has become blood money. Wealth created by the West has fueled his campaigns.

Strategically, the Obama administration made a bet that the deal would spur Iran to stop its rogue state actions and conform to international norms.

That bet was a loser with massive repercussions for all of the people living in the Middle East.

The idea of the JCPOA as a strategic pillar of stability in the Middle East was captured perfectly by John Kerry when he said, quote, "I know the Middle East that is on fire … is going to be more manageable with this deal," end of quote.

Query whether the Middle East is more manageable today than it was when they embarked on the JCPOA.

Lebanon is an even more comfortable home for Hizballah today than it was when we embarked on the JCPOA. Hizballah is now armed to the teeth by Iran and has its sights set on Israel.

Thanks to Iran, Hizballah provides the ground forces for the military expedition in Syria. The IRGC, too, has continued to pump thousands of fighters into Syria to prop up the murderous Assad regime and help make that country 71,000 square miles of kill zone.

Iran perpetuates a conflict that has displaced more than 6 million Syrians inside the—6 million Syrians and caused over 5 million to seek refuge outside of its borders.

These refugees include foreign fighters who have crossed into Europe and threatened terrorist attacks in those countries.

In Iraq, Iran sponsored Shia militia groups and terrorists to infiltrate and undermine the Iraqi Security Forces and jeopardize Iraq's sovereignty—all of this during the JCPOA.

In Yemen, Iran's support for the Houthi militia fuels a conflict that continues to starve the Yemeni people and hold them under the threat of terror.

The IRGC has also given Houthi missiles to attack civilian targets in Saudi Arabia and the Emirates and to threaten international shipping in the Red Sea.

And in Afghanistan, Iran's support to the Taliban in the form of weapons and funding leads to further violence and hinders peace and stability for the Afghan people.

Today, the Iranian Qods Force conducts covert assassination operations in the heart of Europe.

We should remember, too, that during the JCPOA Iran continues to hold Americans hostage: Baquer Namazi, Siamak Namazi, Xiyue Wang, and Bob Levinson, who has been missing for over 11 years.

I will note for the American people, you should know we are working diligently to bring each American missing wrongfully detained in Iran home.

The list continues. Iran continues to be, during the JCPOA, the world's largest sponsor of terror. It continues to serve as sanctuary for al-Qaida, as it has done since 9/11, and remains unwilling to bring to justice senior al-Qaida members residing in Tehran.

Today we ask the Iranian people: Is this what you want your country to be known for, for being a co-conspirator with Hizballah, Hamas, the Taliban, and al-Qaida? The United States believe you deserve better.

And I have an additional point for the Iranian people to ponder. Here in the West, President Rouha and Foreign Minister Zarif are often held apart from the regime's unwise terrorist and malign behavior. They are treated somehow differently.

The West says, "Boy, if only they could control Ayatollah Khamenei and Qasem Soleimani then things would be great." Yet, Rouhani and Zarif are your elected leaders. Are they not the most responsible for your economic struggles? Are these two not responsible for wasting Iranian lives throughout the Middle East?

It's worth the Iranian people considering, because instead of helping their own citizens, the regime continues to seek a corridor stretching from Iran's borders to the shores of the Mediterranean. Iran wants this corridor to transport fighters and an advanced weapons system to Israel's doorsteps. Indeed, in recent months, the IRGC has flown an armed drone into Israeli airspace and launched salvos of rockets into the Golan Heights from Syria. Our steadfast ally has asserted the sovereign right of self-defense in response, a stance the United States will continue to unequivocally support.

So, the bet—the bet that the JCPOA would increase Middle East stability was a bad one for America, for Europe, for the Middle East, and indeed for the entire world. It is clear that the JCPOA has not ended Iran's nuclear ambitions, nor did it deter its quest for a regional hegemony. Iran's leaders saw the deal as the starting gun for the march across the Middle East.

So, the path forward. America's commitment to the Iran strategy President Trump laid down in October remains. It will now be executed outside of the JCPOA.

We'll continue to work with allies to counter the regime's destabilizing activities in the region, block their financing of terror, and address Iran's proliferation of missiles and other advanced weapons systems that threaten peace and stability. We will also ensure Iran has no path to a nuclear weapon—not now, not ever.

Following our withdrawal from the JCPOA, President Trump has asked me to achieve these goals on Iran. We'll pursue those goals along several lines of effort.

First, we will apply unprecedented financial pressure on the Iranian regime. The leaders in Tehran will have no doubt about our seriousness.

Thanks to our colleagues at the Department of Treasury, sanctions are going back in full effect and new ones are coming. Last week we imposed sanctions on the head of Iran's central bank and other entities that were funneling money to the IRGC Qods Force. They were also providing money to Hizballah and other terrorist organizations. The Iranian regime should know that this is just the beginning.

This sting of sanctions will be painful if the regime does not change its course from the unacceptable and unproductive path it has chosen to one that rejoins the league of nations. These will indeed end up being the strongest sanctions in history when we are complete.

The regime has been fighting all over the Middle East for years. After our sanctions come in force, it will be battling to keep its economy alive.

Iran will be forced to make a choice: either fight to keep its economy off life support at home or keep squandering precious wealth on fights abroad. It will not have the resources to do both.

Second, I will work closely with the Department of Defense and our regional allies to deter Iranian aggression.

We will ensure freedom of navigation on the waters in the region. We will work to prevent and counteract any Iranian malign cyber activity. We will track down Iranian operatives and their Hizballah proxies operating around the world and we will crush them. Iran will never again have carte blanche to dominate the Middle East.

And I'd remind the leadership in Iran what President Trump said: If they restart their nuclear program, it will mean bigger problems—bigger problems than they'd ever had before.

Third, we will also advocate tirelessly for the Iranian people. The regime must improve how it treats its citizens. It must protect the human rights of every Iranian. It must cease wasting Iran's wealth abroad.

We ask that our international partners continue to add their voice to ours in condemning Iran's treatment of its own citizens.

The protests—the protests of the past few months show that the Iranian people are deeply frustrated with their own government's failures.

The Iranian economy is struggling as a result of bad Iranian decisions. Workers aren't getting paid, strikes are a daily occurrence, and the rial is plummeting. Youth unemployment is at a staggering 25 percent.

Government mismanagement of Iran's natural resources has led to severe droughts and other environmental crises as well.

Look, these problems are compounded by enormous corruption inside of Iran, and the Iranian people can smell it. The protests last winter showed that many are angry at the regime that keeps for itself what the regime steals from its people.

And Iranians too are angry at a regime elite that commits hundreds of millions of dollars to military operations and terrorist groups abroad while the Iranian people cry out for a simple life with jobs and opportunity and with liberty.

The Iranian regime's response to the protests has only exposed the country's leadership is running scared. Thousands have been jailed arbitrarily, and at least dozens have been killed.

As seen from the hijab protests, the brutal men of the regime seem to be particularly terrified by Iranian women who are demanding their rights. As human beings with inherent dignity and inalienable rights, the women of Iran deserve the same freedoms that the men of Iran possess.

But this is all on top of a well-documented terror and torture that the regime has inflicted for decades on those who dissent from the regime's ideology.

The Iranian regime is going to ultimately have to look itself in the mirror. The Iranian people, especially its youth, are increasingly eager for economic, political, and social change.

The United States stands with those longing for a country of economic opportunity, government transparency, fairness, and greater liberty.

We hope, indeed we expect, that the Iranian regime will come to its senses and support—not suppress—the aspirations of its own citizens.

We're open to new steps with not only our allies and partners, but with Iran as well. But only if Iran is willing to make major changes.

As President Trump said two weeks ago, he is ready, willing, and able to negotiate a new deal. But the deal is not the objective. Our goal is to protect the American people.

Any new agreement will make sure Iran never acquires a nuclear weapon, and will deter the regime's malign behavior in a way that the JCPOA never could. We will not repeat the mistakes of past administrations, and we will not renegotiate the JCPOA itself. The Iranian wave of destruction in the region in just the last few years is proof that Iran's nuclear aspirations cannot be separated from the overall security picture.

So what should it be? We must begin to define what it is that we demand from Iran.

First, Iran must declare to the IAEA a full account of the prior military dimensions of its nuclear program, and permanently and verifiably abandon such work in perpetuity.

Second, Iran must stop enrichment and never pursue plutonium reprocessing. This includes closing its heavy water reactor.

Third, Iran must also provide the IAEA with unqualified access to all sites throughout the entire country.

Iran must end its proliferation of ballistic missiles and halt further launching or development of nuclear-capable missile systems.

Iran must release all U.S. citizens, as well as citizens of our partners and allies, each of them detained on spurious charges.

Iran must end support to Middle East terrorist groups, including Lebanese Hizballah, Hamas, and the Palestinian Islamic Jihad.

Iran must respect the sovereignty of the Iraqi Government and permit the disarming, demobilization, and reintegration of Shia militias.

Iran must also end its military support for the Houthi militia and work towards a peaceful political settlement in Yemen.

Iran must withdraw all forces under Iranian command throughout the entirety of Syria.

Iran, too, must end support for the Taliban and other terrorists in Afghanistan and the region, and cease harboring senior al-Qaida leaders.

Iran, too, must end the IRG Qods Force's support for terrorists and militant partners around the world.

And too, Iran must end its threatening behavior against its neighbors—many of whom are U.S. allies. This certainly includes its threats to destroy Israel, and its firing of missiles into Saudi Arabia and the United Arab Emirates. It also includes threats to international shipping and destructive—and destructive cyberattacks.

That list is pretty long, but if you take a look at it, these are 12 very basic requirements. The length of the list is simply a scope of the malign behavior of Iran. We didn't create the list, they did.

From my conversations with European friends, I know that they broadly share these same views of what the Iranian regime must do to gain acceptance in the international community. I ask that America's allies join us in calling for the Iranian Government to act more responsibly.

In exchange for major changes in Iran, the United States is prepared to take actions which will benefit the Iranian people. These areas of action include a number of things.

First, once this is achieved, we're prepared to end the principal components of every one of our sanctions against the regime. We're happy at that point to re-establish full diplomatic and commercial relationships with Iran. And we're prepared to admit[i] Iran to have advanced technology. If Iran makes this fundamental strategic shift, we, too, are prepared to support the modernization and reintegration of the Iranian economy into the international economic system.

But relief from our efforts will come only when we see tangible, demonstrated, and sustained shifts in Tehran's policies. We acknowledge Iran's right to defend its people. But not its actions which jeopardize world's citizens.

Also, in contrast to the previous administration, we want to include Congress as a partner in this process. We want our efforts to have broad support with the American people and endure beyond the Trump Administration. A treaty would be our preferred way to go.

Unlike the JCPOA, which was broadly rejected across both sides of the aisle, an agreement that President Trump proposes would surely garner this type of widespread support from our elected leaders and the American people.

In the strategy we laid out today, we want the support of our most important allies and partners in the region and around the globe. Certainly our European friends, but much more than that.

I want the Australians, the Bahrainis, the Egyptians, the Indians, the Japanese, the Jordanians, the Kuwaitis, the Omanis, the Qataris, the Saudi Arabians, South Korea, the UAE, and many, many others worldwide to join in this effort against the Islamic Republic of Iran. I know that those countries share the same goals. They understand the challenge the same way that America does. Indeed, we welcome any nation which is sick and tired of the nuclear threats, the terrorism, the missile proliferation, and the brutality of a regime which is at odds with world peace, a country that continues to inflict chaos on innocent people.

Indeed, while to some the changes in Iranian behavior we seek may seem unrealistic, we should recall that what we are pursuing was the global consensus before the JCPOA.

For example, in 2012, President Obama said, quote, "The deal we'll accept is [that] they end their nuclear program," end of quote. That didn't happen. In 2006, the P5 voted at the Security Council for Iran to immediately suspend all enrichment activities. That didn't happen.

In 2013, the French foreign minister said he was wary of being sucked into a, quote, "con game," end of quote, over allowing Iran to continue uranium enrichment.

In 2015, John Kerry said, quote, "We don't recognize the right to enrich," end of quote. Yet the Iranians are enriching even as we sit here today.

So we're not asking anything other than that Iranian behavior be consistent with global norms, global norms widely recognized before the JCPOA. And we want to eliminate their capacity to threaten our world with those nuclear activities.

With respect to its nuclear activities, why would we allow Iran more capability than we have permitted the United Arab Emirates and that we're asking for the Kingdom of Saudi Arabia? We understand that our reimposition of sanctions and the coming pressure campaign on the Iranian regime will pose financial and economic difficulties for a number of our friends. Indeed, it imposes economic challenges to America as well. These are markets our businesses would love to sell into as well. And we want to hear their concerns.

But we will hold those doing prohibited business in Iran to account. Over the coming weeks, we will send teams of specialists to countries around the world to further explain administration policy, to discuss the implications of sanctions we imposition, and to listen.

I know. I've spent a great deal of time with our allies in my first three weeks. I know that they may decide to try and keep their old nuclear deal going with Tehran. That is certainly their decision to make. They know where we stand.

Next year marks the 40th anniversary of the Islamic Republic—Revolution in Iran. At this milestone, we have to ask: What has the Iranian Revolution given to the Iranian people? The regime reaps a harvest of suffering and death in the Middle East at the expense of its own citizens. Iran's economy is stagnant and without direction and about to get worse. Its young people are withering under the weight of frustrated ambitions. They are longing to pursue the freedoms and opportunities of the 21st century.

Iran's leaders can change all of this if they choose to do so. Ali Khamenei has been supreme leader since 1989. He will not live forever, nor will the Iranian people abide the rigid rules of tyrants forever. For two generations, the Iranian regime has exacted a heavy toll on its own people and the world. The hard grip of repression is all that millions of Iranians have ever known.

Now is the time for the supreme leader and the Iranian regime to summon the courage to do something historically beneficial for its own people, for this ancient and proud nation.

As for the United States, our eyes are clear as to the nature of this regime, but our ears are open to what may be possible. Unlike the previous administration, we are looking for outcomes that benefit the Iranian people, not just the regime.

If anyone, especially the leaders of Iran, doubts the President's sincerity or his vision, let them look at our diplomacy with North Korea. Our willingness to meet with Kim Jong-un underscores the Trump administration's commitment to diplomacy to help solve the greatest challenges, even with our staunchest adversaries. But that willingness, that willingness has been accompanied by a painful pressure campaign that reflects our commitment to resolve this challenge forever.

To the ayatollah, to President Rouhani, and to other Iranian leaders: understand that your current activities will be met with steely resolve.

My final message today is, in fact, to the Iranian people. I want to repeat President Trump's words from October. President Trump said that, "We stand in total solidarity with the Iranian regime's longest-suffering victims: its own people. The citizens of Iran have paid a heavy price for the violence and extremism of their leaders. The Iranian people long to reclaim their country's proud history, its culture, its civilization, and its cooperation with its neighbors."

It is America's hope that our labors toward peace and security will bear fruit for the long-suffering people of Iran. We long to see them prosper and flourish as in past decades and, indeed, as never before.

Today, the United States of America is proud to take a new course towards that objective.

Thank you. (Applause.)

MS JAMES: Thank you so very much. Bold, concise, unambiguous. We appreciate you taking this forum here at the Heritage Foundation to deliver that message. Looking at—and you listed during your speech several of our allies and friends and partners, many of whom are angry, some disappointed. How are you going to bring them on board? How are you going to use your best diplomatic skills to bring them along with us?

SECRETARY POMPEO: These strategic changes in the world come together when countries decide on an objective that is shared, and that always begins with a shared interest and values. I spent the first couple of weeks of my time as Secretary of State working to try to see if there wasn't a way to fix the deal. I spoke with my European counterparts. I traveled there. In my 13th hour as Secretary of State I was on the ground in Brussels speaking with my European counterparts. We couldn't get it done. We couldn't reach agreement there.

The United States intends to work hard at the diplomatic piece of working alongside all of our partners. We focus on the Europeans, but there are scores of countries around the world who share our concerns and are equally threatened by the Iranian regime. It's that shared interest, it's the value set which will ultimately drive, I believe, a global response to this—to the world's largest state sponsor of terror. I'm convinced it can take place. My team is going to work diligently to do that. We're going to do so in the context of trying to address the concerns of all of our partners, and I am convinced that over a period of time there will be a broad recognition that the strategy that President Trump has laid out is the right one that will put Iran in a place where it will one day rejoin civilization in the way that we all hope that it will.

Document No. 8: Director of National Intelligence, Worldwide Threat Assessment of the U.S. Intelligence Community, January 19, 2019 [Excerpt]

source: https://www.dni.gov/files/ODNI/documents/2019-ATA-SFR---SSCI.pdf

(The Director of National Intelligence presents an unclassified worldwide threat assessment to Congress annually, representing, in theory, the coordinated views of all 16 intelligence agencies within the US government. These assessments generally support the basic propaganda lines of the Pentagon and the White House on the capabilities and intentions of its four major adversaries. This excerpt reflects the standard U.S. themes of Iranian as regional troublemaker and threat to U.S. and allied interests in the Middle East. It also hints at the possibility of new Iranian military capabilities that could make a U.S. military intervention in the Gulf far more problematic than previously suggested by the Pentagon -- capabilities that were demonstrated dramatically later in 2019.)

Iran

Iran's regional ambitions and improved military capabilities almost certainly will threaten US interests in the coming year, driven by Tehran's perception of increasing US, Saudi, and Israeli hostility, as well as continuing border insecurity, and the influence of hardliners.

Iran's Objectives in Iraq, Syria, and Yemen

We assess that Iran will attempt to translate battlefield gains in Iraq and Syria into long-term political, security, social, and economic influence while continuing to press Saudi Arabia and the UAE by supporting the Huthis in Yemen.

In Iraq, Iran-supported Popular Mobilization Committee-affiliated Shia militias remain the primary threat to US personnel, and we expect that threat to increase as the threat ISIS poses to the militias recedes, Iraqi Government formation concludes, some Iran-backed groups call for the United States to withdraw, and tension between Iran and the United States grows. We continue to watch for signs that the regime might direct its proxies and partners in Iraq to attack US interests.

Iran's efforts to consolidate its influence in Syria and arm Hizballah have prompted Israeli airstrikes as recently as January 2019 against Iranian positions within Syria and underscore our growing concern about the long-term trajectory of Iranian influence in the region and the risk that conflict will escalate.

Iran's retaliatory missile and UAV strikes on ISIS targets in Syria following the attack on an Iranian military parade in Ahvaz in September were most likely intended to send a message to potential adversaries, showing Tehran's resolve to retaliate when attacked and demonstrating Iran's improving military capabilities and ability to project force.

Iran continues to pursue permanent military bases and economic deals in Syria and probably wants to maintain a network of Shia foreign fighters there despite Israeli attacks on Iranian positions in Syria. We assess that Iran seeks to avoid a major armed conflict with Israel. However, Israeli strikes that result in Iranian casualties increase the likelihood of Iranian conventional retaliation against Israel, judging from Syrian-based Iranian forces' firing of rockets into the Golan Heights in May 2018 following an Israeli attack the previous month on Iranians at Tiyas Airbase in Syria.

In Yemen, Iran's support to the Huthis, including supplying ballistic missiles, risks escalating the conflict and poses a serious threat to US partners and interests in the region. Iran continues to provide support that enables Huthi attacks against shipping near the Bab el Mandeb Strait and land-based targets deep inside Saudi Arabia and the UAE, using ballistic missiles and UAVs.

Domestic Politics

Regime hardliners will be more emboldened to challenge rival centrists by undermining their domestic reform efforts and pushing a more confrontational posture toward the United States and its allies. Centrist President Hasan Ruhani has garnered praise from hardliners with his more hostile posture toward Washington but will still struggle to address ongoing popular discontent.

Nationwide protests, mostly focused on economic grievances, have continued to draw attention to the need for major economic reforms and unmet expectations for most Iranians. We expect more unrest in the months ahead, although the protests are likely to remain uncoordinated and lacking central leadership or broad support from major ethnic and political groups. We assess that Tehran is prepared to take more aggressive security measures in response to renewed unrest while preferring to use nonlethal force.

- Ruhani's ability to reform the economy remains limited, given pervasive corruption, a weak banking sector, and a business climate that discourages foreign investment and trade.

Military Modernization and Behavior

Iran will continue to develop military capabilities that threaten US forces and US allies in the region. It also may increase harassment of US and allied warships and merchant vessels in the Persian Gulf, Strait of Hormuz, and Gulf of Oman.

- Iran continues to develop, improve, and field a range of military capabilities that enable it to target US and allied military assets in the region and disrupt traffic through the Strait of Hormuz. These systems include ballistic missiles, unmanned explosive boats, naval mines, submarines and advanced torpedoes, armed and attack UAVs, antiship and land-attack cruise missiles, antiship ballistic missiles, and air defenses. Iran has the largest ballistic missile force in the Middle East and can strike targets as far as 2,000 kilometers from Iran's borders. Russia's delivery of the SA-20c SAM system in 2016 provided Iran with its most advanced long-range air defense system. Iran is also domestically producing medium-range SAM systems and developing a long-range SAM.

- In September 2018, Iran struck Kurdish groups in Iraq and ISIS in Syria with ballistic missiles in response to attacks inside Iran, demonstrating the increasing precision of Iran's missiles, as well as Iran's ability to use UAVs in conjunction with ballistic missiles.

- We assess that unprofessional interactions conducted by the Iranian Islamic Revolutionary Guards Corps (IRGC) Navy against US ships in the Persian Gulf, which have been less frequent during the past year, could resume should Iran seek to project an image of strength in response to US pressure. Most IRGC interactions with US ships are professional, but in recent years the IRGC Navy has challenged US ships in the Persian Gulf and flown UAVs close to US aircraft carriers during flight operations. Moreover, Iranian leaders since July have threatened to close the Strait of Hormuz in response to US sanctions targeting Iranian oil exports.

Document No. 9: Statement from the National Security Advisor Ambassador John Bolton, May 5, 2019

source: https://www.whitehouse.gov/briefings-statements/statement-national-security-advisor-ambassador-john-bolton-2/

(National Security Adviser John Bolton introduced a new crisis atmosphere into U.S. Iran policy in early May 2019 by announcing a claim of evidence of new Iranian military threats to U.S. personnel and allies in the Middle East, none of which was based actual intelligence findings.)

In response to a number of troubling and escalatory indications and warnings, the United States is deploying the USS Abraham Lincoln Carrier Strike Group and a bomber task force to the U.S. Central Command region to send a clear and unmistakable message to the Iranian regime that any attack on United States interests or on those of our allies will be met with unrelenting force. The United States is not seeking war with the Iranian regime, but we are fully prepared to respond to any attack, whether by proxy, the Islamic Revolutionary Guard Corps, or regular Iranian forces.

About the Authors

Gareth Porter is an investigative historian and journalist specializing on the U.S. national security state. He has covered dozens of exclusive investigative stories about U.S. policy in U.S. wars and military operations in Vietnam, Iraq, Afghanistan, Pakistan, Yemen and Syria and U.S policies toward Iran. He is author of five books, including *Perils of Dominance: Imbalance of Power and the Road to War in Vietnam* (University of California Press, 2005) and *Manufactured Crisis: the Untold Story of the Iran Nuclear Scare* (Just World Books, 2014).

John Kiriakou is a former CIA counterterrorism officer, former senior investigator for the Senate Foreign Relations Committee, and former counterterrorism consultant for ABC News. He was responsible for the capture in Pakistan in 2002 of Abu Zubaydah, then believed to be the third-ranking official in al-Qaeda. In 2007, Kiriakou blew the whistle on the CIA's torture program, telling ABC News that the CIA tortured prisoners, that torture was official US government policy, and that the policy had been approved by then– President George W. Bush. He is the author of multiple books on intelligence and the CIA.